'To the Land of the Free from this Island of Slaves'

Henry Stratford Persse's Letters from
Galway to America, 1821–1832

IRISH NARRATIVES

IRISH NARRATIVES
Series edited by David Fitzpatrick

Personal narratives of past lives are essential for understanding any field of history. They provide unrivalled insight into the day-to-day consequences of political, social, economic or cultural relationships. Memoirs, diaries and personal letters, whether by public figures or obscure witnesses of historical events, will often captivate the general reader as well as engrossing the specialist. Yet the vast majority of such narratives are preserved only among the manuscripts or rarities in libraries and archives scattered over the globe. The aim of this series of brief yet scholarly editions is to make available a wide range of narratives concerning Ireland and the Irish over the last four centuries. All documents, or sets of documents, are edited and introduced by specialist scholars, who guide the reader through the world in which the text was created. The chosen texts are faithfully transcribed, the biographical and local background explored, and the documents set in historical context. This series will prove invaluable for university and school teachers, providing superb material for essays and textual analysis in class. Above all, it offers a novel opportunity for readers interested in Irish history to discover fresh and exciting sources of personal testimony.

Other titles in the series:

Andrew Bryson's Ordeal: An Epilogue to the 1798 Rebellion, edited by Michael Durey
Frank Henderson's Easter Rising, edited by Michael Hopkinson
Memoirs of Joseph Prost: A Redemptorist Missionary in Ireland, 1851–1854, translated and edited by Emmet Larkin and Herman Freudenberger

Forthcoming titles:

A Patriot Priest: A Life of Reverend James Coigly, edited by Dáire Keogh

'My Darling Danny': Letters from Mary O'Connell to her son Daniel, 1830–1832, edited by Erin I. Bishop

David Fitzpatrick teaches history at Trinity College, Dublin. His books include *Politics and Irish Life, 1913–1921* (1977) and *Oceans of Consolation: Personal Accounts of Irish Migration to Australia* (1995).

'To the Land of the Free from this Island of Slaves'

Henry Stratford Persse's Letters from Galway to America, 1821–1832

Edited by
James L. Pethica and James C. Roy

CORK UNIVERSITY PRESS

First published in 1998 by
Cork University Press
Cork
Ireland

10 9 8 7 6 5 4 3 2 1

British Library Cataloguing in Publication Data

A CIP catalogue record for this book is available from the British Library.

ISBN 1 85918 141 4

Typesetting by Red Barn Publishing, Skeagh, Skibbereen

Printed in Ireland by ColourBooks, Baldoyle, Co. Dublin

Contents

Acknowledgements

The bulk of the letters in this volume are preserved in the collection of Persse family materials assembled by the late Mr John Windsor Persse, of Hamden, Connecticut — a great-great-grandson of Henry Stratford Persse — and his wife, Mrs Mary Louise Persse. We are particularly grateful to Mrs Persse for making them and much additional material available to us, for her encouragement and support towards our project, and for the many kindnesses both she and her son, John Windsor Persse III, extended to us during the course of our work.

Mr Thomas Persse of Fonda, New York, generously made three additional letters available to us. Our thanks to Mr and Mrs Richard Persse of Crailinghall, Roxburghshire, for making available family materials in their possession. Elizabeth Moyer and Schuyler Persse of Johnstown, New York, were most helpful in tracking down genealogical details.

We are most grateful to Professor David Fitzpatrick, who read our first draft and offered numerous valuable criticisms and suggestions for the project both then and at many later points in its development for the *Irish Narratives* series. Our best thanks also to Professor Roy Foster, whose generous encouragement, criticisms and suggestions after reading our first draft were invaluable. Joe O'Halloran shepherded an article based on a portion of the Introduction into print in the *Journal of the Galway Archaeological and Historical Society* with meticulous care and very kindly allowed us to reuse transparencies prepared for that printing. The Rev. James Mitchell generously sent us corrections and supplementary information during our work on that article.

Henry Stratford Persse's correspondence with DeWitt Clinton is reproduced by kind permission of Columbia University. Our thanks to Patrick Lawlor of the Rare Book and Manuscript Collection at Columbia for his assistance. We would also like to acknowledge the assistance of: Rev. Eustas Ó hÉideain, O.P., and Patrick Ryan of University College, Galway; Blake McClenachan; Professor Mary Ellen Cohane of North Adams State College; Brigadier K. A. Timbers of the Royal

Artillery Historical Trust; Maurice Semple; T. A. Heathcote, Curator of the Collection at the Royal Military Academy, Sandhurst; Wade Wells of the New York State Museum Cultural Education Center; Professor Julie Roy Jeffrey of Goucher College; Ruth Bonito, Associate Curator of the Windsor Locks Historical Society; Robert Sullivan and Howard White of the Windsor Historical Society; John Ryan of Haverhill, Massachusetts; Dr John Howe, University of Minnesota; Maureen Moran, Galway County Library Headquarters; Ms Alex Ward, Curator of the Grand Lodge of Ancient, Free and Accepted Masons of Ireland. Our grateful thanks also to the staffs of: the National Library of Ireland; the Colindale Newspaper Library, London; the Connecticut State Library Archives; the Connecticut Historical Society; the Montgomery County Historical Society; the Johnstown Library; the State Archives and Records Administration of SUNY, Albany, New York; the Williams College Computing Center; the Holyoke Public Library.

Our thanks also to Professor Maureen Murphy and Professor Lucy McDiarmid, who generously supported a grant application towards our work on this project, to Tom Wong, whose inputting of our first transcription of the correspondence got our work off to a speedy start, and to Rob Ellis, who proof-read the final copy with exemplary care.

Introduction

The Great Famine of 1845–49 has inevitably loomed large as the *terminus ad quem* in assessments of Irish economic and social conditions of the early 1800s. To many of those who escaped the starvation and fever that claimed around a million lives, the Famine was a consequence as much of longstanding British apathy and exploitation as of simply the failure of the potato crop. For them, and for many in subsequent generations, 'Famine Queen' Victoria and the *laissez-faire* ideology of Lord John Russell's Whig administration became focal points of bitter race-memory, and the Famine itself was remembered as a disaster that should have been easily foreseen and hence forestalled. In recent years, however, historians have increasingly emphasised that our knowledge of the pre-Famine period is fragmentary and ambiguous at best. Although contemporary accounts provide abundant testimony to widespread poverty for the overwhelming majority of Irish labourers and cottiers in the 1820s and 1830s, the causes of these conditions, and, equally important, contemporary attitudes towards them among the Irish landlord and mercantile classes, have become matters of considerable controversy. Most recently Cormac Ó Gráda has urged an explicit guard against the potentially distortive effects of viewing the period through the lens of the crisis that followed. 'That something like the famine was quite unimaginable to contemporaries may seem implausible to later generations, conditioned by Malthusian inference and nationalist rhetoric,' he writes, in a striking reminder of the academic tendency to 'write history backwards'. Despite that implausibility, he concludes, 'evidence that life was becoming progressively more precarious in the pre-Famine decades is scarce, no matter how persuasive the retrospective case'. For the vast majority, he argues, the potato blight indeed arrived 'like a thief in the night', to bring a devastation that was unprecedented in scale precisely because it was so unanticipated.[1]

The letters which comprise this volume, written in the 1820s and 1830s from Galway city, voice the opinions of one remarkable man for whom the impending crisis was far from 'unimaginable', a man who urged strenuously as early as 1822 that the potato, 'the root of misery', should be 'abolished from the *general* use of Irishmen'(L6).[2] His sense of urgency, moreover, went far beyond simply warning against the dangers of over-reliance on a single agricultural resource. Recognising the corrosive effects of complacency and dissipation in the landowning Ascendancy class, the widespread corruption and divisiveness in Ireland's political and religious institutions, and the lack of economic vigour in his culture generally, he foresaw a general collapse in the structures of Irish life if the *status quo* were to remain unchanged. Acting resolutely on his convictions, he encouraged three of his younger sons to emigrate to America in 1821, subsequently sending out at least four other sons by 1830. His letters to them, spanning the years 1821 to 1832, articulate the hopes of a man deeply enamoured of the meritocratic principles of American democracy, but also the frustration and resignation of a man who recognised that for himself it was too late to leave 'this Island of Slaves' (L3). Well-educated, determinedly entrepreneurial and pragmatically liberal-minded, he remained in Galway until his death in 1833, fighting a rearguard action to improve conditions locally. His letters record a wealth of social detail from the Connacht of the 1820s, include first-hand accounts of the famines and political upheavals of the period, and provide a vital insight into early attitudes towards emigration. Most importantly, they constitute a remarkable critique of the Irish landowning and Ascendancy class, and of the prevailing structures of economic and political power, by a member of that very elite he saw as being at the root of Ireland's ills.

The Past

> When Dean Dudley Persse purchased Roxborough for a trifle he was called a mad man to quit Dublin and go to the *wilds* of Connaught. (L12, January 1825)

I

Henry Stratford Persse (HSP) was born *circa* 1769, the fourth son of William Persse, a prominent Connacht landlord. William Persse's estate at Roxborough, County Galway, situated at the foot of the Slieve Aughty mountains some twenty miles south-east of Galway city, was an oasis of prosperity in otherwise poor terrain little changed since his great-grandfather, Dean Dudley Persse, had first purchased land there 'among wolves and other wild beasts' a century earlier and been thought a 'mad man' (L12) for doing so. Galway city aside, eighteenth-century Connacht was a sparsely populated region lacking roads, settled agriculture or significant mercantile activity, in which many of the smaller settlements were but the meanest assemblage of hovels, peopled by a poor and often illiterate peasantry struggling under subsistence conditions. Well into the nineteenth century English travellers would record vignettes of Connacht life so wretched as to inspire both 'compassion and disgust'.[3] Demesnes such as Roxborough, at its peak a holding of over 12,000 acres, occupied the richer champaign lands of the central Galway plain, whose value the Normans too had recognised, as scores of ruined towers and keeps testify to this day. Ascendancy landlords like William Persse ruled these demesnes as they saw fit, determining — with varying degrees of liberality or harshness — the conditions of life for a tenantry separated from them by the bounds of religion and often language, as well as wealth.[4]

The Persse family, along with their Protestant Ascendancy neighbours — the Eyres, Blakeneys, Lamberts, Galbraiths and Clanricardes — were more than just rural gentry. At the time of Henry Stratford's birth these few landowners held every position of power in the county: they ran the constabulary, attended grand juries, officered local militias, and served as sheriffs. Persse family members alone, for instance, filled the position of sheriff of Galway on thirteen occasions between 1701 and 1899.[5] And as a class, the Ascendancy dominated commercial affairs in Galway city, in the 1760s still a substantial commercial port and mercantile centre, though already entering into a commercial decline that would leave it by the century's end in a state of 'neglect and decay' and 'almost proverbial for uncleanliness and inconvenience'.[6] In agricultural matters they instigated varied and often visionary schemes of improvement on their lands, from breeding better stock and improving methods of cultivation to draining bogs. In step with this pre-eminence came their overwhelming control of the local Catholic populace, who served them as workmen, farriers, blacksmiths, tillers, gardeners, masons, herders, domestics, dairymen, and tenants in general. In times of unrest the Ascendancy could, and often did, resort to the protection of Crown forces, but with the exception of occasional insurrections, their control of both the land and positions of social and economic influence in the region ensured stability to their dominance.

The Persses were not indigenous to the Connacht landscape, nor did they claim to be, even after several generations of tenure at Roxborough. From the earliest times of recorded history Connacht had been the home to an assortment of Celtic clans — the O'Kellys, O'Shaughnessys, O'Heynes, and others, all of whom were overshadowed to some degree by the monarchial O'Connors, one of whom claimed the high-kingship of Ireland when Norman warriors first appeared on the island in 1169. The Normans, in the main rough and unregenerate freebooters, waged battle with the native population, and later with each other, for over two centuries, in a more or less continuous struggle for control of the land, a conquest never fully won. In the span of just eighty years many initial Norman successes had been virtually eliminated through intermarriage, fosterage or treaty with native Irish dynasties. By 1335 the premier Norman family in western Ireland, the de Burgos, had been thoroughly absorbed into local culture, becoming in many respects indistinguishable from the 'mere Irish' so deplored in the Statutes of Kilkenny. Even so, Henry de Burgh, twelfth Earl of Clanricarde, who in 1782 came into his inheritance of estates totalling 50,000 acres in Connacht alone, could still trace direct descent from William de Burgo who had been granted the province by King John in 1195. The Clanricardes, and many families like them, had once been known as the 'Old English', in recognition of both their Catholicism and their status as pioneers. The blood spilt in battles for control of the region marked a bond with the landscape of County Galway that freshly arrived adventurers, known as the 'New English', could never hope to equal.

II

The term 'New English', broadly defined, signifies the horde of settlers and speculators who descended on Ireland from the sixteenth century. These were, famously, the years of religious dissension as Henry VIII, and later his daughter Elizabeth, broke with Rome, precipitating the great cleavage of Europe into opposed religious camps. As has often been noted, these were exasperating times for England and horrific ones for Ireland. Elizabeth, parsimonious yet demanding, unleashed ambitious and hardened men upon the land who sought to extend English authority, and with it English law, custom, language, taxes and, most significantly, religion, to a country and people unused to tightly fettered control. The results were often bloody, and in Galway particularly so. Roving bands of soldiers, no matter the parochial cause or allegiance, routinely destroyed whatever lay in their path. Records of butchery, though apparently commonplace for the age, still vividly manage to evoke images of horror to those reading them today. Attitudes hardened at the court in London as military forays became ever more costly in money, lives and reputations. 'Ireland do break their hearts, it is now grown to such a misery,'[7] wrote one observer of the English; but in however creaking a fashion, Elizabeth did, in the end, prevail. The battle of Kinsale in 1601, its results not finalised for another hundred years until William of Orange triumphed at the Boyne, was a devastating defeat for Catholic Ireland, one from which it would never wholly recover.

For many of the soldiers in Elizabeth's armies, payment for their services came in the form of land, and estates that had been won by the sword or confiscated were portioned out and soon occupied by waves of settlers. In their wake came speculators like the fabulously successful Richard Boyle, first Earl of Cork, and an assorted melange of hangers-on, businessmen, charlatans, thieves, investors and clergymen. Robert Persse, who arrived on Irish soil around 1602, came as a 'Minister of God's Word'.[8]

Little is known of Robert's background, personal or educational, other than a vague family tradition that he came from Northumberland. In later years, as the Persses prospered, genealogical connections were hypothesised to the noble house of Percy (Shakespeare's Hotspur), and their coat of arms and motto, *Esperance en Dieu*, were duly appropriated. Robert's Irish career, a span of about nine years, was certainly modest. Ecclesiastical records indicate that he managed to secure three livings within the Pale which provided a comfortable, if not lavish income.[9] His son Edward inherited one of these upon Robert's death in 1612 and added two others that same year, both of which he held until 1641,[10] when much of his property was swept away in the great convulsion of rebellion that broke out initially in Ulster. A deposition signed by Edward records in pitiless detail the plight of many a Protestant gentleman during those perilous times. Turmoil in England between Charles I and parliament had encouraged the wildest rumours of an imminent rising in Ireland by disaffected papists. Many landowners of small means such as Edward Persse sought to hedge their property with sympathetic Catholic neighbours. In Edward's case he entrusted twenty-seven head of 'English breede' cattle worth £79 and a variety of domestic goods ('one great chest full of Lynnen, three great Brasse Potts, one feather bed, three great Brewing Pans, and household stuff with all necessaryes and appurtenances')[11] into the care of neighbouring Catholics. These possessions simply disappeared as rebellion engulfed the country, Irish and Old English alike slipping into treason. At one point a mob of local ruffians broke into Edward's vicarage at Capoch and 'there did disposeth, despoyle, robb, and deprive of all'.[12] Among those recognised at the scene was one William FitzGerald, an alleged friend with whom Persse had placed nine of his cattle.

Edward Persse, of course, was not alone, as Protestant ministers were particularly choice targets for sectarian outrage. Many more eminent clergy suffered ruin of far greater proportion than Persse's modest losses. Archbishop Ussher — Primate of All Ireland, antiquarian, confidant to the king — saw his various estates and country seats burnt to the ground and utterly destroyed. He chose never to reside in Ireland again, living the remainder of his life in penury in England. Edward Persse, it is thought, died in 1643. He would have been in his early fifties.

III

The decade from 1641 to 1651 was perhaps the most tumultuous of any in the long saga of Irish history, culminating in the exploits of Oliver Cromwell and his New Model Army, which virtually extinguished the Old English tenure of Irish land. It has been estimated that Catholic ownership of property fell from 59 per cent in 1641 to only 22 per cent forty years later, a percentage inflated somewhat by minor restorations when Charles II, with Catholic sympathies, was restored to the throne. After the Boyne, however, Catholics found themselves almost totally dispossessed. Only 14 per cent of Irish land was held by Catholics at the turn of the eighteenth century, and that by far the poorest.[13] These proved to be splendid years for opportunists.

The Rev. Dudley Persse, it must be said, was one of these. The third generation of his family to take holy orders, he is the first about whom we know anything substantial regarding background and personality. In the year 1641 his father (Edward's younger brother) enrolled Dudley in Trinity College, Dublin, at the age of sixteen. Trinity, founded by Elizabeth I fifty years before, was a bastion of Protestant sensibility from its very inception, a common ground where the future leaders of Ascendancy Ireland could meet and study in complete isolation from the papists they were groomed to rule over and enlighten. The upheavals that had ruined Edward Persse, however, disrupted his nephew Dudley's education to such measure that he did not receive a degree for some twenty years. By then he had married and sired most or all of his nine children to survive infancy.

Dudley's later prosperity seems to have largely derived from friend-ships he made at Trinity. For many years he preached at St Michan's, a parish at the epicentre of seventeenth-century Dublin's considerable suburban growth, and in which some of Ireland's most elaborate ducal mansions would be built. Dudley Persse can be seen about the fringes of this burgeoning society. Sponsored from within the Established Church by clergymen more prominent than himself, he managed to cultivate the attention of powerful Protestant landowners such as Ormond and the Earl of Drogheda, and the results were tidy from both quarters. After gaining his degree in 1661, he was collated to several livings: Fenmore, near the bishopric of Clonfert; Taghsaxon in County Galway; the deanship of Kilmacduagh in County Galway; and the archdeaconry of Tuam in Mayo. On the secular front, he received grants of land, most of them small, in both Roscommon and Galway from Charles II and later his successor, James II, all to the wonderment of a nineteenth-century Catholic historian, who labelled him 'fortu-nate, if not distinguished'.[14]

In fact both labels were probably justified. Dudley Persse did exhibit the nerve and aggressive pragmatism so often associated with the New English breed of entrepreneur. Connacht, scene of so much disaffection and rebellion over the centuries, was never judged as anything but a risk. Dean Dudley may well have taken livings that no one else cared to assume, for his farmlands meant nothing if spoiled each year by roving bands of Catholic marauders. But he was clearly a man of ambition. Local legend subsequently had it that his acquisitiveness on occasion went beyond the bounds of legal risk. After Roxborough was burnt dur-ing the troubles of 1922, locals descended on its smouldering ruins to sift through the debris in search of church plate that Dean Dudley had allegedly appropriated and hidden on the property generations earlier.[15]

That the Rev. Dudley Persse intrigued for ecclesiastical preferment is certain, as a letter dated 10 October 1682 to an acquaintance of the Duke of Ormond testifies. 'I am of the opinion that ere long there will be an opportunity,' he wrote, 'for the Archbishop of Cashel is almost at death's door. He cannot live many days. I was in those parts about ten days since and he was very weak. Upon his death I know there will be removals and then it will be, I presume, a fit time for his Grace to appear, and if you please to be a remembrancer to his Grace in my behalf I shall owe it with all thankfulness and, upon the success, manifest my gratitude. Pardon this trouble I beseech you.'[16] Energetic place-hunting was an accepted feature of Dean Dudley's culture, but even to his contemporaries this nakedly predatory appeal must have seemed to be overstepping the mark: at all events, his lugubrious death-watch over the tottering archbishop went unrewarded. A surviving portrait of the dean does little to contradict the impression of blunt opportunism suggested by such surviving documentary evidence. As Elizabeth Coxhead noted in her biography of Lady Gregory — the most distinguished of the later Roxborough Persses — a twentieth-century descendant of Dean Dudley 'cheerfully' acknowledged that the portrait conveys 'the expression of a thorough scoundrel'.[17]

The nucleus of the Persse estate lay along the Owenshree river, to the west of a low ridge of boggy hills that run from the market town of Loughrea in County Galway in a south-easterly direction to the shores of Lough Derg on the Shannon. Here, during some period in the last third of the seventeenth century, Dean Dudley Persse built a residence on the land known as 'Cregroostha', an Irish name that was subsequently anglicised to 'Gregerosty' and finally to 'Roxborough', according to family legend in deference to their Northumbrian origins.[18] By the time of the dean's death in 1700 the holding consisted of forty-seven acres, but his eldest son Henry sold off his father's peripheral lands and purchased in their stead nearly six hundred adjoining acres from the former Duke of York's estate, auctioned off by parliament to pay bills left over from the Boyne, Aughrim and Limerick. Over three or four generations Roxborough was extended to 12,000 acres, with the Persses becoming noted for their prowess as graziers and wool dealers. Dean Dudley's modest Jacobean seat was gradually transformed into a large if undistinguished country mansion, said to have been the first slate-roofed house in the county.[19] Separate branches of the family flourished in the region, settling Castleboy, down the road from the main house of Roxborough, Moyode Castle, near the ancient Norman frontier town of Athenry, Belleville, further north towards Mayo, Lime Park, and numerous other demesnes. By 1800 combined Persse holdings would number some 25,000 acres.[20]

However impressive such statistics might sound, it would be a mistake to imagine that the world into which Henry Stratford was born rivalled that of landholding gentry in Great Britain itself, or even in the Pale. Connacht was a decided backwater, and while Roxborough itself was almost completely self-sufficient as an estate, providing food, drink, clothing and employment, it generated only modest amounts of surplus cash. The Persses were prosperous enough to pursue the family sport of fox-hunting with some exuberance, but they were no match to the grandees of Ireland, men like the Earls of Clanricarde, who were sent to the best schools in England, travelled widely throughout Europe, kept mansions in Dublin and London, and served in upper-echelon government positions. The influence and pursuits of the Persses, were, by contrast, almost entirely local in scope. Whereas the Earl of Clanricarde provided tremendous copy for the gutter press of London — 'He was now obliged to lower his tone, and address her only as a Platonic lover, though he burnt with the most violent passion to possess her',[21] and so forth — the scandals affecting the Persses were those common to the relatively isolated rural gentry: drunkenness, sloth, addiction to the hunt or card games in a local village, the occasional illegitimate child. The few published accounts of the habits and tastes of the late eighteenth- and nineteenth-century Persses have promoted a Jonah Barrington portrait of hard-drinking, rowdy and often ruthless landlords. Primed by Lady Gregory, whose disaffection with her parents left her with a lastingly critical attitude towards the family, W. B. Yeats included in his *Autobiographies* a colourful narrative of the devil-may-care exploits of the Persse menfolk ruling their demesnes with 'despotic benevolence': they had been 'soldiers, farmers, riders to hounds, and, in the time of the Irish Parliament, politicians . . . but all had lacked intellectual curiosity'.[22] Later accounts have closely followed Yeats's lead. Elizabeth Coxhead, for instance, stressed that Roxborough had been a 'totally unbookish house' and judged that if the Persses were probably 'no worse than the general run of Anglo-Irish landlords: at best it is always a sorry story'.[23] Mary Lou Kohfeldt writes more sensationally of 'rumours of the seduction of maids and country women' and recounts local memories of a Persse son said to have boasted 'that he did everything that could be done out of the way except kill a man'.[24] Such accounts amply capture the least impressive strands of nineteenth-century Persse accomplishment, but at the expense of recognising an earlier, more enlightened period in the family's history. Between the thrusting pioneer opportunism of Dean Dudley Persse and his immediate progeny and the dissipations of some later generations, the eighteenth-century Persses had briefly enjoyed a considerably more cultivated and intellectual tradition, and it was into this that Henry Stratford Persse himself was born.

IV

Henry's father, William Persse, master of Roxborough for some three decades before his death in 1801, represented the high point in this phase of Georgian enlightenment. Well connected through his mother's and paternal grandmother's families, he seems to have been groomed for success, rising to High Sheriff of Galway at the unusually early age of thirty-eight. Born around 1728, he was in his prime during the period of social and political turmoil precipitated by the start of the American Revolution in 1775. For William Persse, as for many other Ascendancy landlords, the American cause of self-determination struck a strong chord. Though some in his immediate family circle seem to have taken a determinedly loyalist stance — his brother-in-law William Blakeney, for instance, was wounded fighting 'rebels' at Bunker Hill, while his younger brother Henry served for more than a year on American soil with British forces — for Persse himself, Ireland's lack of political representation in the imperial parliament, and its grievances at British restrictions on and taxation of Irish trade, offered an acute and telling parallel to the colonial conditions against which America had risen. His pro-American views met with encouragement from many friends and neighbours. His close associate Sir Edward Newenham, for instance, was a staunch enthusiast of the American cause, building a monument to George Washington on the grounds of his estate in 1778, complete with an inscription that read: 'O ill-fated Britain! the folly of Lexington and Concord will rend asunder and forever disjoin America from the Empire.'[25] Newenham's eldest son, William, subsequently married William Persse's daughter Elizabeth, thereby cementing their ties on a family basis.

In the wake of the revolution, William Persse emerged as a major instigator of the Volunteer movement in the west of Ireland, following closely on the example of his maternal cousin Sir William Parsons (whose family name Henry Stratford Persse later gave his fourth son as a first name). Originally raised as militia replacements for standing troops destined for service in North America, the early Volunteer groups were conceived as broadly loyalist in allegiance, guarding against civil disturbance and possible invasion. From the outset, however, the movement provided a forum for men of independent views. As Roy Foster has remarked, the act of Volunteering inevitably tended to foster a spirit of 'citizenship, of "patriotism", of exclusive [Irish] identity',[26] while the sense of military autonomy and responsibility for regional interests that local corps quickly gained likewise called into question the nature of those rights and privileges for whose defence they had ostensibly been formed. Under the command of William Persse, the 'Roxburrow Volunteers' were in the vanguard as the movement gradually began to take an ever more explicit nationally-minded complexion in the later 1770s. Reviewing a group of Volunteer corps in Galway city in 1781, for instance, 'Colonel Persse', as he was now styled, presented an address to the Earl of Clanricarde which expressed the Volunteers' intention to 'rescue this defenceless country' both 'from the dangers which awaited it from surrounding enemies' — an orthodox intention — and, more pointedly, 'from the unjust fetters which [have] bound its inhabitants so long as to make this favoured soil of Heaven the residence of poverty and oppression'.[27] The language of colonial dissent is strong here, but the source of oppression significantly remains implied rather than named. By the following year, however, the nationalist demands of the Volunteers for legislative independence from Britain were laid out explicitly and defiantly in a series of resolutions passed at Dungannon and approved by a March regional meeting of Volunteers at Ballinasloe which appointed William Persse to key regional committees. Drawing self-consciously on the American Declaration of Independence, the resolutions included the proposition

> That no power on earth has a right to make laws to bind this kingdom, except the King, Lords and Commons of Ireland, and that we will resist, with our lives and fortunes, the execution of other laws, as we consider to be governed by a foreign legislature over which we have no control — *absolute slavery*.[28]

Echoing this carefully phrased call for autonomous Irish rule a month later in his triumphant address to the Dublin parliament, Henry Grattan ushered in the eighteen years of nominal legislative independence known as 'Grattan's Parliament'. To celebrate the new political dispensation, codified early in 1783, William Persse emulated his friend Newenham's penchant for monuments by building a small 'Volunteer' bridge on the Roxborough estate, with a commemorative plaque, which still remains, inscribed: 'This Bridge was Erected by / William Persse Esquire, Colonel of / the Roxburrow Volunteers in / The Year 1783 / in Memory of Ireland's / Emancipation From Foreign / Jurisdiction'.

The later record of William Persse's life suggests that the example of American democracy continued to shine as an ideal for him well after the brief triumphs of 1783. As a landlord he appears to have been considerably more liberal in outlook than his Ascendancy neighbours. In 1786, for instance, he declined to sign two strongly worded declarations of intent by local landowners to prosecute and evict tenants who attended Whiteboy meetings.[29] A tribute published in Galway some thirty years after his death remembered him as a tolerant man, who though 'a *Protestant*, descended from a *Protestant* family, [and] conscientiously attached to the principles of that creed, [was] not one of those believers who pin their political faith upon the sleeves of "the powers that be", and who hold it as a maxim that "whatever is, is right"'.[30] Religiously open-minded (he entertained a reluctant John Wesley at Roxborough in 1785), he viewed the traditional sectarian divisions of Ireland as negatively as its political institutions.

Reflecting this spirit of idealism and his continued pro-American zeal is the evidence of his correspondence with George Washington. The single exchange of letters which survives was initiated by Persse in 1786, following a visit from Newenham, who was a frequent correspondent with Washington. Hearing of Washington's interest in plant husbandry, Persse sent a gift of gooseberry plants to Mount Vernon along with instructions for their care ('Put a good deal of rotten dung into each hole before you plant them', and so on). America, he remarked in closing, 'is the country of all on earth I long most to see; it would give me new life and vigour to see the upright and honest men of America. Give me leave, dear Sir, to assure you I have been, in the worst times, your well-wisher and a sincere friend to the liberties of America.'[31] Washington, in turn, replied with a formal note of thanks. In letters included in this volume Henry Stratford Persse gives the impression that substantial further correspondence passed between his father and the general and that a cordial friendship developed between the two men. Given that Henry Persse was a young adult at the time, his remarks probably reflect first-hand memories. Washington certainly sent Persse at least one gift, a glass-enclosed case of stuffed birds, later destroyed in the Roxborough fire of 1922, and a brief note from Persse to Washington regarding a business matter, dated 1796, survives in the Library of Congress, but it is uncertain now how many other letters actually passed between the two men.[32] Regardless, it is clear that William Persse revered Washington and all he stood for. The general's portrait hung in his drawing-room at Roxborough, and he named his summer lodge on the Burren coast 'Mount Vernon' in his honour. As we shall see, Henry Stratford Persse would absorb much of his father's enthusiasm for Washington, and for the American republic, without reserve.

For all the heady idealism and celebrations of 1783, though, William Persse died a disappointed man. By the last years of the century he had come to recognise that nominal independence was insufficient to reform the Irish parliament. In the wake of the 1798 uprising and the Act of Union in 1800, the latter engineered by Pitt using bribery and patronage the likes of which contemporaries had never witnessed, the brief hope for reform melted irrevocably away. It must have been with mixed feelings of pragmatic resignation that he eventually added his name in 1799 to a Galway petition urging union with Great Britain: 'We are of opinion that uniting our strength in the closest manner with the wisest, freest, and the happiest people upon earth, with whom we must necessarily stand and fall, is so far from a sacrifice of the honour and independence of Ireland, that it is the best means left to us for preserving both.'[33] He was to die two years later, in 1801.

The Present

Nothing but misery all around me (L8, January 1823)

I

As a younger son in a large family Henry Stratford Persse had no immediately attractive prospects ahead of him as he grew into manhood, and none at all at Roxborough itself, willed entirely to his first-born brother, Robert, a bequest that ensured for that lucky man the life 'of a luxuriant idler' (L6). As for so many younger sons of landlords, a familiar range of choices beckoned — a military or engineering career, perhaps placement in the legal profession, or most likely of all a minor post in county government. The course of his early life, though, is uncertain. He refers in one letter to learning the business of weaving in Cork as a young man, and may have been sent to learn various such business skills by his father as a preparatory phase to starting out as an entrepreneur, much as he would subsequently encourage his own sons to learn business skills as apprentices. At some point relatively early in life, however, no doubt through the influence of his father, he secured the post of Landwaiter in the customs house of Galway, a position which entailed documenting arriving cargoes and levying the appropriate duties. It was not the top job in the profession, being ranked below the largely sinecure positions of Collector and Port Surveyor, but it was a position of considerable responsibility and social standing. He appears to have held the post for most of his adult life, and is still listed as 'Landwaiter' and additionally as 'Searcher and Coastwaiter' in the 1830 edition of *The Treble Almanack*, published three years before his death.

His government salary, some £700 per year by the 1820s, placed him as a gentleman of solid means on the social and economic scale of his day, but it was a sum that had to meet ever-growing needs following his marriage to Anne Sadleir in 1792, as she bore him twenty-two children, of which ten sons and two daughters survived infancy. Ever intent on bettering his lot, and congenitally an entrepreneur by nature, HSP engaged in various commercial ventures to supplement his income. The most significant of these was a brewery and distillery which he founded in 1815 on Nuns' Island in Galway city, and he also established a substantial grain-milling operation around 1810.[34] Between 1818 and 1826 he was Postmaster for Galway, a largely honorary position which brought in an additional £59 5s per year.[35] The success of these ventures helped consolidate his position as a man of substance in Galway society, a position reflected in his lease of Newcastle House, set in fine grounds overlooking the River Corrib on the western side of Galway city and listed by James Hardiman in 1820 as one of the main 'country seats' in the area.[36] True to form, however, he remained a man of frugal means. There would be no expensive thoroughbreds in his stables or ostentatious display in his household, and his letters give the impression of a practical man always resistant to the seductions of class display and self-indulgence. When he did enjoy country sports, he would do so in the same fashion as local tenants and peasants: on foot with a dog or two, rousting after rabbits.

II

Henry Stratford Persse's surviving letters begin in 1821, when their author was in his early fifties. Aside from a handful written to DeWitt Clinton, Governor of New York in the 1820s, they are addressed to three of his sons who had emigrated to the United States. Dudley, Richard and Theophilus Persse settled first along the Hudson River Valley, pursuing careers in agriculture and the paper trade with mixed success. One eventually served a term in the Connecticut sate legislature. Their various progeny slipped into the mainstream of American society, some heading west to Colorado, others attending Ivy League schools and entering the professions. The family correspondence was preserved by the generations of descendants who remained on the homestead established by Theophilus in Johnstown, New York.

The historical value of the letters is primarily threefold: the sharp insights they provide into conditions in Galway during a period of famine and significant economic and social tension; the acute critique they offer of Irish political and religious institutions; and the record of contemporary attitudes to America and emigration that they provide. At their heart, though, is the engagingly maverick personality of their author, and the hopes he entertained for his sons. The central dynamic of his writings is an alternation between pragmatic disillusion over Irish affairs and mercurial optimism for the potential of American democracy. Like many educated men of his class, Persse looked fondly backwards to the idealism of 1782, and believed that rational self-government by enlightened Protestants could bring prosperity and political stability to Ireland. The chance for reform, though, had come some thirty years before, and in his view had now clearly passed. 'The accounts from Limerick and Cork are beyond description,' he laments in a letter of February 1822. 'No man's life is there safe. It is a regular war between the oppressors and the oppressed, and in this scene of human carnage, I dare say you would not wish to earn a laurel at *either* side.' Against the miseries of contemporary Ireland, he held fast to the vision of American meritocracy and opportunity he had inherited from his father. He saw himself as too advanced in life and habit, too burdened with the cares of family and position, to think of emigrating himself, but his advice to those with youth and ambition was: leave now!

At their father's urging, Dudley, Richard and Theophilus, the oldest about twenty years of age, the youngest fifteen, sailed for America in August 1821. The three sons were among the early waves of what would become a torrent of emigrants as the century progressed. The flight of some three million Irish to Great Britain and America in the quarter-century following the onset of the Famine in 1845 should not obscure the fact that emigration had long been a commonplace in Irish life. Celtic saints and *peregrini* such as Columcille, Columbanus and many hundreds of other less fabled missionaries had institutionalised the abandonment of Erin as the *oilithreacht gan tiontú*, or 'pilgrimage without returning', while the many celebrated partings of subsequent history — from the Flight of the Earls to the peregrinations of the Wild Geese — had long been been a mainstay of Irish lore and song. To leave the 'honeyed greens' of Ireland, to walk away from hearth and kinfolk, was considered by every Irish-speaking peasant with immense foreboding. For those of the Protestant minority, however, whether middle-class tradesmen from Ulster or younger sons of Ascendancy landlords, such nostalgia was secondary to more practical and commercial considerations. During the 1700s and the first third of the nineteenth century, according to Kerby Miller, for every Catholic who emigrated, three Protestants took ship for abroad, and it was not until the 1840s, with the Famine and its economic aftermath, that Irish Catholics began to dominate the wholesale exodus that would continue throughout the remainder of the century.[37]

For Henry Stratford Persse, more prescient and incisive in his economic thinking than most of his Ascendancy contemporaries, and less subject to necessity than the Catholic underclass, the justification for urging his sons to leave 'this terrible system' (L3) was both commercial and political. As he pointed out to them, 'I have not been an idle observer in life' (L9), and with conditions deteriorating in his native land he had acted resolutely in trying to improve their lot. By 1821 the boom of the Napoleonic wartime era had long ended. Ireland, commercially dependent on British mercantile policies, had suffered severely from the collapse in grain and livestock prices on the one hand, and competition from English manufactured goods on the other. With no parliament of its own to protect Irish interests through tariff or duty provisions, the country slipped gradually into economic crisis from 1815 onwards, a situation exacerbated by the levying of new taxes following the amalgamation of the Irish and English exchequers in 1817 and by widespread outbreaks of typhus fever. Landowners, in particular, felt enormous pressures as the value of their estates fell, rent rolls shrunk, and mortgage payments fell in arrears.[38] Commenting on the fortunes of one of Connacht's premier families, the Lamberts of Castle Lambert in northern Galway, Persse noted that they hadn't £5 in ready cash to their name (L8). As conditions deteriorated, many landlords resettled either in Britain or Europe to avoid taxes, accelerating the phenomenon of absenteeism that was already endemic at the beginning of the century. As Persse reported to his sons in April 1822, 'distress is fast increasing, and many wealthy families are gone to France to live'. Locals, he noted, had begun to wonder 'how any one that has any means to quit would live in the vagabond climate of Ireland among our overtaxed, famishing cut-throat people'. In addition to listing prominent landlords who had recently left either temporarily or permanently, Persse also stressed that 'working people' were emigrating if they could: 'One ship put in here from Dublin has upwards of 360 passengers on board bound for Quebec. So you see that rich and poor are running away from the rents and the tythes and the taxes, and God help them that must stay at home and pay *their* share and their own share till they come back' (L5).[39]

As a younger son who had had to build prosperity by his own efforts, Persse readily understood the limited prospects for advancement that faced his own boys if they stayed. His four eldest sons, William, Henry, Robert and Parsons, at this point in their early to late twenties, were all sources of disappointment and frustration to him, showing little inclination to pursue with any vigour the various careers he recommended — including positions in the Post Office and the East India Company — relying instead on allowances from their father and any other relatives with means. His letter of February 1822, in particular, rails at length against the lack of initiative in these four 'lick plate' sons and their complacent willingness to remain 'a burthen upon me' (L3). He was consequently determined that his younger sons, still teenagers, should not linger in the corrupting influence of Ireland.

As it was for all emigrants, whether Catholic or Protestant, peasant or landlord, the physical voyage to America was a dangerous prospect, and the enormous ampitheatre of the New World almost overwhelming in its contrast to the provincial society of Galway. Persse's early letters betray the anxiety he suffered over their trans-Atlantic journey, voicing fervent thanks for their safe passage over the 'perilous deep' (L2), while for his wife, who was initially convinced that they had been shipwrecked, the strain of worry and parting continued even after she heard of their safe arrival — 'Dudley in the yellow fever at New York is all her cry' (L7). But in marked contrast to the pathos that separation from Ireland produced in most Irish peasants, Henry Stratford welcomed their departure. There is no lugubrious lament over 'exile' or 'banishment' from Erin to be found in his letters, only the firm belief that through industry and working hard with their hands on the level field of endeavour that 'Yankee Land' provided, their chances for success were inevitable. Expounding on the admiration of his father for Washington's republic, Persse saw America in almost hallowed terms. Where Ireland was 'vagabond', commercially enslaved, beset by agrarian and sectarian violence, ruled in a corrupt fashion by landlords and feudalists, America was a 'free country' where one's fate was 'in your own hands. Apply, study, gain the ability to reach the top of the wheel, and there is no law human or *divine* in force in *America* that can stop you from taking the palm' (L9). Neither mounful nor melancholic, nostalgic nor snared in the past, Persse viewed the New World, to use Kerby Miller's description, in 'entrepreneurial' terms, and those who returned to Galway after failing in America stunned him by their want of energy and application.[40]

III

The political idealism and enthusiasm for American democracy which HSP had inherited from his father were merely the most visible aspects of a profound liberalism that informs his critique of political and social structures throughout these letters. That he was a Protestant there can be no doubt. His attitudes were clearly those of an educated and observant member of the Ascendancy class. But although he denigrated Catholicism now and again in passing, his references are neither virulent nor sectarian. As a self-pronounced man of reason, in fact, he was most concerned to criticise examples of 'papist' authority and ostentation within the ruling hierarchy. Judges in their robes and wigs, for example, pronouncing death sentences at sessions in Cork, Limerick and Galway, disgusted him with their display of 'mummery' and their undue influence as much as any 'Priests and Bishops dressed out at High Mass' could have done. Whether in religion or politics, it was always the gap between real and assumed abilities, and the corrosive impact of nepotism and 'interest' in regulating social status, that irritated him most:[41]

> I do not see why mummery and nonsense should be retained or attached to our Courts of Law, no more than to our Church. But the fact is, that Interest makes Judges too, and to cover the blockhead it is necessary to give him some imposing dress so as to obtain for him that respect which his want of knowledge disentitles him to. And thus it is that these chaps are dressed out like Popish Priests to keep the ignorant in awe. (L5)

In fact his contempt for the Established Church and the tithes levied to support it was pronounced. Protestant clergymen, drawn too often from 'the faro table, the mess room, the staff, the brothel, the Navy and the kennel . . . wallowing in the champagne of Paris or the *Lachrimae Christi* of Naples', disgusted him (L7). In Persse's scheme, a man's dignity was directly related to the utility and energy with which he worked. However humble his profession, a man should gain credit and respect for carrying out his duties honestly, not because of the wealth or influence he had attained.

Consistent with this view, Henry Stratford never subscribed, as so many of his Ascendancy contemporaries did, to a monolithic and dismissive view of the Catholic peasantry. Poor and illiterate they might often be, but in his view the vicissitudes of history and the mismanagement of Ireland were more the cause than any inherent lack of worth. His liberalism was put to its most severe practical test during the Galway Famine of 1822, when he acted on his convictions by taking a central role in organising local relief. At the height of the distress, when the sight of people 'dying like rotten sheep' in the streets of Galway left him barely able to contain his anger at a system of '*Paternal* government' that tolerated starvation while corn was exported from the port he oversaw, he and his wife took in five emaciated children who had been 'left in the street like birds in the snow to perish' (L6). While others of means had refused to help the children for fear of being infected with typhus fever, the Persses carefully nursed them to recovery. Even in their half-starved condition, HSP could acknowledge their humanity, remarking that the eldest child was 'so like' his own son Theophilus in manner. The lasting consequence of the episode was that the second youngest of the children, three-year-old Polly Geary, was kept as a ward of the household, with her charm, vitality and imagination quickly captivating all who saw her. 'Just now pause and reflect,' HSP told his boys. 'Here was a little female child, that if educated and taken care of had all the essentials to be a Queen, left like a deserted cat to perish in the streets, and this is the system that is "the envy of surrounding nations and the admiration of the World"' (L6). Though Polly Geary could speak only Irish when first taken in, she was within weeks able to 'speak English as well as she did Irish before', learned 'her *small* letters . . . in one day' and displayed a natural taste and quickness that both astonished Persse and acted as a constant reminder to him of the inequities everywhere in Ireland:

> I never saw that gentleman's child that has such pretty manners . . .
> this Polly Geary is the Child that the aristocracy would fain make us

believe was a *different species* of the human race, 'papist devils that nothing could civilize or amend'. Oh Ireland! what a country you would be today if you were governed, my Dear Boys, in the way you know I would wish. (L7)

His response to such wastage of human potential was focused, as was invariably his way, on political and practical solutions — solutions that he necessarily assumed must come first from those in a position of influence within his own class. Consequently — and regrettably, given the liberalism and incisiveness of his insights — we can catch only glimpses of the full breadth of his views about indigenous Irish culture in these letters. He seems, for instance, to have been able to understand Irish to a high functional level, an unusual accomplishment for an Ascendancy Protestant of his time, apparently conversing easily with both Polly and her eldest brother, and even using an occasional phrase himself in writing to his sons. His pleasure in the folklore retailed by Polly Geary likewise hints at openness to peasant beliefs, an openness also suggested by his high regard for the work of Lady Morgan, whose novels insist on the value and integrity of Irish culture. Resolutely practical in his focus, though, HSP seems to have wasted little if any time in musing over the broader cultural consequences of the social and economic inequities he observed, and it would have to wait until his grand-niece, Lady Gregory, learned Irish and began collecting folklore in the 1890s that the talent for easy exchange across boundaries of religion, language and class that he seems to have embodied would find its fullest familial outlet and literary focus. For Henry Stratford Persse, the essential facts were that the great mass of Catholic Irish-speaking peasants were in essence nothing more than 'truly oppressed and distressed and heartbroken white slaves', wilfully and shamefully neglected by the Ascendancy elite (L9).

IV

In almost every one of his surviving letters Persse identifies the perpetrators of that neglect: the landed gentry, a class of 'strolling idler[s]'

(L12) to whom 'the dirt under your feet is more valued than the sweat of man's brow' (L7). As a younger son, of course, he had cause for bitterness, and the incessant critiques of the evils of primogeniture in his letters are obviously coloured at times by resentment. Whereas his eldest brother lived a comfortable existence as a landed squire, counting his rents and generally lacking obvious motivation or accomplishment, Henry himself was often pressed to exhaustion by his government and business responsibilities. Though a resolute believer in the dignity of 'sweat', it is clear that he was frequently pressed to the point of extreme exasperation. But even worse, in his view, than the complacency which landed inheritance tended to foster was the pervasively infecting example of that langour in Ascendancy culture as a whole. Acute examples of indolence and nepotism abound in his commentaries, but no idleness disappointed him more than that of his own eldest sons, all in danger of becoming ne'er-do-wells. The three boys in America, shovelling manure and labouring like honest men, were the source of his pride; the others, wasting away to 'hereditary indolence', were his shame (L7). His letters repeatedly alternate between anger and lament for lost opportunity as they survey these sons' irresolution. William 'gives himself too much to the bottle ever to reform and now I see no hope whatever of his getting any situation'. Henry 'is worse', the result of a brawl over cards for which 'he received a fine painted face so bad that he could not show for ten days. I certainly will turn him out of the house.' 'I know not what Parsons is about' (L6). His third son, Robert, a 'boy . . . full of the pride of idleness' who 'never comes near us but once . . . the last twelve months' (L6) was the prime offender, though, giving himself the airs of a gentleman though without any means to sustain the impersonation:

> Robert wants to get to be a Barony Constable under the new act . . .
> a man employed to hunt down the peasantry and see that they are in
> their houses after sunset, and not out before sunrise . . . [to] force
> them to pay rent, tythes, and taxes. A fine trade for what is called a
> Gentleman (L6) . . . He is only fit to be a driver over slaves. He

would not for £500 a year spoil the shape of his nails by any unfashionable occupation. (L8)

Persse saw all this as symptomatic of the degraded state of Ascendancy society, 'priding in the insolence of their birth' (L7). In his long letter of 22 July 1822, ever ready to turn his criticisms to some practical benefit, he took the opportunity to impress upon his emigrant sons their good fortune in leaving for America, and thereby justify having urged them so strenuously to emigrate:

> You see what an inroad upon industrious pursuits is created by a previous habit of indolence . . . [This] urged me to remove you from the dire effects of such example, well knowing from experience myself that my happiest days were those wherein I was most actively engaged. And seeing that this country held out *no hope* of your doing good here, I hastened you off to the land where four corner chat is not the custom and where labour, whether of the body or of the mind, is the true representative of wealth, and not land. (L7)

V

The backdrop of an unspoiled America framed the three major areas of disaster that Persse saw enveloping his native land, each of which he addresses at considerable length in his letters: the destruction of Ireland's economy; agrarian violence; and the scourge of famine and fever. All three were in his view interrelated, and each incapable of remedy under the existing political dispensation. At the heart of his critique of the *status quo* was a belief that the deflationary monetary policies of Great Britain were strangling any chance for meaningful progress in Ireland. His views draw broadly on radical contemporary social commentary, but perhaps most obviously on the writings of William Cobbett. Cobbett, who rose from ploughboy to prominence, eventually becoming a member of parliament, was in most respects the very image of the kind of self-reliant, self-improving and critical mindset Persse aspired to both for himself and his sons. In a series of recent works Cobbett had repeatedly challenged the prevailing structures of privilege, emphasised the real extent of poverty and social inequity in Britain and Ireland, and offered self-help advice for small farmers and entrepreneurs. Persse forwarded a number of such 'improving' texts to his emigrant sons, including Cobbett's newly published volume *The American Gardener* — advice concerning the propagation and cultivation of crops — in his letter of July 1822. It seems probable that he was also familiar with Cobbett's pivotal essay *Paper Against Gold*, a swingeing critique of contemporary monetary policy, as his arguments frequently seem to be inspired by Cobbett's. Using the circulation of the blood as his central image for monetary exchange, for instance, he offers an extended attack on current taxation policies and the debilitating effect of deflationary forces:

> Money, or circulating medium as it is called, is like blood in the human body. If you stop or even contract the circulation, debility follows. Money is not food, yet all starve without it . . . Blood to appearances as a fluid contains no strength in it, yet bleed the strongest man plentifully, or stop the circulation of that blood, and no infant so weak as he is immediately. (L6)

The obstructing factors that had lessened the flow for the Irish economy, bringing it both metaphorically and actually to a state of famine, were in his view 'tythes, rents, and taxes', a suffocation which struck rich and poor alike (L6).

All classes had been adversely affected by the agricultural depression that commenced with Napoleon's defeat in 1815. Prices collapsed just as rents, ironically, began rising. Competition for available land among a soaring population grew intense, particularly for peasant farmers whose only blessing, it seemed, was that 'darling root' (L5), the potato — nutritious, easy to grow, and requiring very small plots to cultivate. Competition from English markets had ruined many Irish producers and crushed individual initiative, but at the heart of the problem, for Persse, were the crippling excise taxes and duties, such as he was himself obliged to impose daily in his work at the Galway Customs House:

> Robert Lambert . . . is most anxious to join you [in America], but I believe his father could not raise £5 to fit him out. No wonder. Mr. Lambert had fifty acres of wheat this year. If he wants a ton of iron, he must give two tons of wheat to pay for the *duty* of the iron, one ton of wheat to pay the tax or duty upon one ton of timber, one hundred weight of wheat to pay the tax upon one deal plank or a pound of tea, five hundred weight of wheat to pay for the *duty* upon one hundred weight of sugar. He gives four hundred weight of wool where his father gave but one, to pay the duty on wine, and he will now get but one gallon of whiskey at a grocery store for a fat sheep. If he or his tenants want *tobacco* they must give a good ewe to pay the duty upon one pound of tobacco, or fifty-two stone of potatoes, or ten stone of oats, or ten horseloads of turf . . . everything *here* that we can *see*, *feel*, *touch*, or *understand is taxed*, and now, my Dear Boys, do you wonder that Mr. Lambert, although having an estate in this country, should be without five pounds to send out his son to you? (L8)

In his usual manner, Henry Stratford tried to turn adversity to advantage in this long letter of despairing complaint, assuring his sons that 'it was not to draw your attention to the hardship of *his* case that I stated it, but to show in clearer colours the advantages you possess'. The 'misery and woes' they had escaped, however, were too overwhelming even for his pragmatic mind to easily contain, and he ends resignedly admitting the level of his personal distress: 'I will disgust you no more with this hateful Subject, for its effects create such terrible misfortunes, and these before my eyes every day, that I cannot work them from my mind.'

Out of such calamity, not surprisingly, came agrarian outrages. Landlords, pressed for money to service interest debt on often heavily mortgaged estates, began evicting a tenantry that had often paid its rent in kind or in labour. Secret societies like the Whiteboys sprang up, maiming livestock, assaulting land agents and at times subjecting entire counties to lawless reigns of terror. Persse's correspondence recounts with exasperation the resulting killings and retributory hangings that were routinely reported in the local press. His sympathies in this scene of turmoil were most certainly not with the privileged, for while he could write regretfully about the ruin of small farmers and the beggarly condition of the peasantry, he tartly follows an observation that landlords were 'without rents' with the comment 'God be praised' (L8). Violent resistance to the misery he saw 'all around' was in his view the inevitable response to oppression, and coercion likely to make matters only worse:

> The County of Cork is again disturbed as is part of Limerick, Tipperary, Kilkenny, and Clare. When was it otherwise? And when will it be that the rat which is squeezed in the dog's mouth to the point of death, will not bite and turn upon his destroyer, although he knows that his doing so only hastens his own destruction. I need not tell you my Boys the causes of these disquietudes. You know why it is that the men of rank and property barricade their houses, and travel with guards and firearms in this country, and do not in yours. (L7)

In Ireland, he noted, every corner of the country crawled with 'soldiers, peelers, revenue police, and waterguards'. In America, his sons had reported, there was no standing army. 'I am glad you have seen no soldiers,' he wrote. 'Man is prone to peace' (L6).[42]

VI

The one great leveller, the one phenomenon that, in Persse's opinion, might persuade the ruling elites that they shared at least some interests in common with the peasant underclass, was the famine which ravaged Connacht in the 1820s and the 'pestilence' that travelled in its wake. Reliable evidence of the extent of distress described by HSP in the Galway region in 1822 is scant, as few local newspapers earlier than 1824 have survived, and previously available personal testimonies give limited indications as to the extent of mortality.[43] During the cholera epidemic of 1832, for instance, which he alludes to in his final letter in this edition, detailed accounts of urban mortality were compiled and published in the daily press by the newly established Central Board of Health, even if rural areas were still often overlooked.[44] For the Galway distress of 1822, however, Persse's accounts are an important addition to an otherwise fragmentary record, written by one who was at the heart of local relief operations.[45]

His long and generally harrowed letters begun on 1 April and 10 July 1822 (both of which were composed in fits and starts, with almost daily entries, as he awaited the next sailing for America) provide an acute and affecting record of the course of the tragedy and his part in trying to limit it. The prospect of widespread starvation, which he had already recognised as likely in March that year, emerges as an ever starker actuality as these letters progress. Potatoes, priced at 7½d a stone on 7 April 1822, are by 20 April 8d, by 5 May 9d, and by 10 July not to be obtained at any price. Hardships recorded in the early portion of the first letter soon give way to extreme distress, and by July Persse describes personally attending to the feeding of 1,500 starving families, all of whom were 'townspeople', while '3,000 strangers' from the countryside were barely kept alive by other food distributions. His account of Galway city describes 'hundreds of families that wander about, pale, emaciated, those whom hunger has rendered appalling, and whom famine has devoured to the very bones and ligaments', and includes telling details of despair, to be repeated a generation later, of the starving eating thistles and seaweed — with fatal consequences — in their efforts to survive.

Although Persse participated in the meetings organised by local committees to co-ordinate relief efforts, he evidently held out little hope of finding kindred minds, sharing his sense of urgency, in these organisations. After describing in his letter of 10 July the dismal scenes at the food distributions he oversaw each day — the press of hungry people resulting in 'legs and ribs broken' — he dimisses the work of the committees with sceptical brevity: 'Here we have long debates, in which I take no part, as long speeches to hungry bellies is but bad food.'

As far as relief from British parliamentary sources was concerned, however, he recognised the value of active engagement and successfully can-
vassed for relief works to include roads of real utility, linking local
communities and along which the 'mail coach' could subsequently
travel, rather than the building of useless follies such as would prevail
in the relief efforts of the 1840s. Utilitarian projects, he believed,
would ultimately bring some benefit, but in general he regarded the
relief efforts of the authorities in London and the work schemes most
often approved as entirely inadequate. Whereas the family governess in
writing to the boys in America would obsequiously praise 'the great
and liberal exertions of the English nation for which Irishmen will ever
bear grateful recollection', Persse was full of disdain:

> English generosity has interposed and sent relief, and what relief is
> it? Some of the same food that in our poverty, early this season we
> were obliged to send away though we knew we should want in the
> Spring. But what does all this generosity amount to? A few thousand
> pounds sent here to relieve the starving people. Why send any? Why
> not leave the people their own? Give me the duties or taxes paid by
> Pat Joyce or John Kelly and Stephens, and I would make more
> improvements and give more relief than all that will be done here
> with English generosity and the munificence of a *Paternal* govern-
> ment. (L6)

The inescapable and offensive truth at the heart of the famine was, as
Persse put it, 'the riddle' of 'people starving in the midst of abundance'. His correspondence provides a grisly and prophetic view of the
misgovernment that would have even more tragic consequences in the
greater catastrophe of 1845–49.

While the victims of famine and '*Paternal* government' were invariably the poor, Persse took an ironic form of comfort from the fact that
the fever that came in its wake made no discriminations along the lines
of class or political leanings. His letters mention numerous members of
the Ascendancy, and indeed some relations, being stricken, usually
fatally, by typhus. It is a telling index of the extent of his rage at human

culpability for the famine that he could see the democratic impact of the contagion as perversely beneficial:

> Yesterday morning, at half past four o'clock, your Aunt Persse died of the fever . . . Great as her loss to the poor, the poor will benefit by her death. Let them pine in decay, jaundice, bile, dropsy, dysentery, sore legs, venereal, or in short any complaint but what is *contagious*, and there is no relief afforded to them. But to save the rich of fever that they might take from the poor, a fever hospital is built here, but no other is thought of. An infirmary for the cure of broken bones they think ridiculous, as the calamity is not contagious. Now it was the famine that brought the fever, that is well known, and the one being coupled with the other, or following its heels, is a blessing, for if it were the case that the people could die as in other cases without affecting the lives of the rich by contagion, then they might rot unheeded and nothing would be done to save their lives . . . What a state it is, that an evil must be created to raise up a benefit in this unfortunate land. (L6)

This passage is one of the blackest and most hopeless in tone of any in Persse's correspondence. Though typhus was the great leveller, it served merely to highlight how entrenched the politics of self-interest were in his culture, and how limited the prospects for any lesson being learned from its devastating impact.

VII

Henry Stratford Persse knew the state of Ireland to be profoundly flawed, but while he saw the reform of political and social institutions as the dominant necessity, he was also prescient enough to realise exactly where the greatest potential for immediate ruin lay — the potato, 'the 'root of misery' as he called it (L6). His father had been an energetic improver as a landlord; it was their joint interest in agricultural innovation, 'so beautiful and pleasing a study', that had been the focus of his correspondence with George Washington. Like his contemporary Richard Gregory at nearby Coole Park, who built up a library well stocked with the latest publications on drainage, husbandry and new techniques in planting,[46] Henry Stratford Persse was eager to maintain his father's enlightened interests in this field as well. In his important letter of 10 July 1822 he details for his sons the causes of the current food shortage and lays out a prophetic vision of the dangers of over-reliance on a single crop:

> As Mr. Yates thinks my ideas about the root of misery strange, coming as they do from the only Irishman who has ever exclaimed against potatoes, I think I am called upon to reply and explain my reasons for wishing to see this root abolished from the *general* use of Irishmen. Potatoes require great manure and tillage. The best lands and the greatest portion of dung is used in their cultivation. Lands that we give to wheat or oats without any manure are appropriated to this culture. The crop when raised acre for acre does not contain (although *bulk* says the contrary) as much nutricious aliment as wheat or oats, and if an unpropitious season follows one that had been superabundant, the whole people starve, for who ever heard of potatoes of even the former year being available to meet or supply the defect in a present one? Can potatoes like wheat, oats, barley, rice, or Indian corn be held over for even fifteen months to make up the deficiency in a short crop? If they could, where could stores be got to lay by the unwieldy article? Not so with corn and grain. They can be preserved for *many years* and lie in a small compass too. So the famine of one year may be guarded [against] by a hoard in the previous one. (L6)

What Persse called the 'Potato Standard' — the correlation between agricultural wages and the price of potatoes — in his view inevitably drained the peasantry's ability to make ends meet in times of poor harvest. If the potato crop should fail, as in 1822, peasants who had been 'fed upon the lowest scale of human sustenance' would have no recourse to a cheaper food. Even if there were a surplus of other, more expensive crops, as was indeed the case in 1822, potato-reliant communities would be left starving. 'Can he who has been fed and paid by the scale of the root of misery all of a sudden *ascend* to bread, beef, and beer? No, he cannot. And although these may be, as they are now, in superabundance, he may starve in the midst of plenty, as is the case this moment all around me.' Once again, however, Persse seems to have been resigned to the improbability of his warnings being heeded, and he turns from the subject with the limited hope that his sons might at least persuade their American host that his arguments were valid.

VIII

The pessimism about Ireland which marks Persse's letters is rarely relieved. If the social and political *status quo* were not enough of a depressant on his spirits, the climate was 'vagabond' and the people 'cut-throat' (L5). But Persse took great solace in looking westward to the idealised republic he had staked his sons' futures on, and in turning to this more congenial subject-matter he displays the elasticity of mind and optimism that domestic events had weighed down. He was clearly an affectionate father, and his long newsy letters to his 'Darling Boys' attest to his generosity of spirit, showing him organising siblings to include notes of their own with his long journal-style missives, bundling reams of newspapers and pamphlets for shipment to New York City, and sending seeds, lambs and money to help further their agricultural fortunes.

This emotional and material largesse reflects some of the dominant functions HSP evidently hoped the correspondence would serve. As David Fitzpatrick has remarked in *Oceans of Consolation*, his compendious study of mid- and late nineteenth-century correspondence between Irish emigrants to Australia and the family and friends they left behind, 'letters provided almost the only instument for maintaining connections with separated relatives'.[47] The parent of twelve children, and himself the product of a culture in which the kinship ties of extended family networks intricately bound by intermarriage were essential to both social and professional success, HSP took his responsibilities for maintaining the bonds of family very seriously. His letters repeatedly urge his sons to write more often, and express vigorous frustration and disappointment when any 'chasm in our correspondence' developed. In part, the letters were obviously motivated by the desire to obviate the sense of loss he felt in having sent away his favourites, and to reduce his sense of separation from them. As he muses in Letter 6, 'my pen cannot be taken from my Boys as it is the only mode I have of conversing with them'. He was irrepressibly eager for news of life in 'Yankee Land', urging his sons to send him descriptions of farming conditions and prospects in the various trades, of the social habits of Americans, portraits of the freemen to whom they were indentured, and details of all the aspects of everyday life — from public matters such as bear-hunts, husking parties and ploughing practices, to the *minutiae* of their domestic lives such as details of their meals, furnishings, and so on. No detail was to small if he was to be able to 'see' the new lives they were leading: 'Unless we can learn all this from you we never can be at home with you' (L8).

At the same time, the letters were also designed to sustain his parental authority and the guiding moral influence he saw as at the heart of his responsibility as a parent. Almost every letter offers some kind of formalised advice: about the evils of 'interest' and primogeniture, about the dignity of labour and self-sufficiency, the duty to help one's own, and, latterly, the necessary conditions for successful marriage. Clearly schooled in the epistolary traditions of the late eighteenth century, in which a moral *exemplum* was an expected element in the letter form — we can safely assume that he had read Samuel Richardson's novels and epistolary guides, for instance — HSP seeks repeatedly to instil and sustain a strong sense of personal duty, both to himself and the family, in his writings. Unable to supervise their development personally, he again and again urges them to take example and guidance from the most 'frugal, industrious, sturdy, and systematic' (L9) around them — their 'dear Uncle' Richard Sadleir for instance, and after he proved unreliable, Theophilus's father-in-law, Mr Edwards — and to concentrate on developing their own characters as upstanding and productive citizens. 'Man being an imitative animal', he writes, 'adopts the forms and customs in which he sees those around him brought up in . . . You may be therefore assured that it is nearly a truism that man may be judged of by the company he keeps and that he forms his character from the circumstances that he is associated with' (L9).

HSP's efforts to maintain emotional ties and to retain moral influence were, of course, intimately interlinked. At times his requests for information reflect an obvious anxiety as to whether he had done the right thing in sending them away, and a need for reassurance that his idealised vision of America held substance. The return of two local emigrants in 1822, full of criticism of America, rattled his composure and inspired him to write several hundred words of heavily rhetorical denunciation of conditions in Ireland. Again, when a Persse family emigrant returned in 1825, leaving the area 'big with story' from 'the lies he circulates', Henry Stratford's contempt seems nervously excessive, culminating in his hope that 'the blackguard will enlist . . . be sent abroad and we shall never hear his name mentioned again' (L12). At the root of any such anxiety was the fear that his sons might fail, and be forced to return to Galway in a fashion that would humiliate them and shatter his own hopes. Again and again his letters urge them to strenuous and honest effort and offer them a support mixed with a call to obligation: 'Far as I am away, I know my advice will be listened to' (L12).

That support, and his eagerness for information, are both evident in Persse's wholehearted efforts to acquaint himself as best he could with the culture his sons had adopted. He followed American political events, and particularly the politics of New York State where his sons were based, with careful attention. As we shall see, his correspondence with Governor DeWitt Clinton reflects a knowledge of current New York affairs that must have relied on considerably more reading than simply the political columns of the Irish press. Indeed, in the only surviving portrait of HSP he is holding a copy of the *New York Herald*.[48] The letters show him attentive to any possible source of information about the New World, reading American travel books by Richard Darby, Frances Wright and others, and studying maps of upper New York State, the better to advise his sons Richard and Theophilus in their plans to purchase farms along the Erie Canal. Their style too gives every sign that Persse was generally an active and careful reader. The letters are articulate and well crafted, studded with many allusions to writers, politicians, distant places of interest and current events. Drawing on diverse literary models, from Cobbett to Swift, whose pamphlets obviously inform the style of some of his more splenetic and rhetorical political paragraphs, they show an easy and unpretentious familiarity with a broad range of recent literature, and show that for all his preference for pragmatic matters of business and practicality he remained an eager scholar throughout his life.

The largesse and intellectual breadth the letters display in their contents is paralleled by their material form, with Persse's free-flowing and expansive hand covering up to 71 pages of script in the longest surviving letter, and the writer making no effort to be 'frugal' with the spacing of his text. Such extravagance is a rarity in surviving correspondence from the period, owing to the exorbitant cost of sending mail. The two decades before the introduction of the penny post in 1840 were a period of notorious inefficiency, during which already substantial postal charges began to rise to prohibitive levels. Both in Britain and Ireland — whose postal systems remained separately administered long after the Act of Union — mail was charged according to distance, with the recipient rather than the sender paying the cost. A single letter of minimum weight — a single sheet — travelling between Dublin and Galway in 1814 cost 9d, while a similar letter from the west of Ireland to London cost around 2s, charges which remained at or above these levels through the 1820s.[49] Such sums were, of course, not only well beyond the reach of the literate among the labouring class — whose wages, as HSP mentions here, ranged from '4 pence to 10 pence per day' (L6) — but also beyond the regular means of even the majority of those above the subsistence level. For mail directed overseas the costs were greater still, and there was considerable added risk. Letter 17 refers to the loss of one cargo HSP had sent to the hands of an unscrupulous sea captain, and he anxiously inquires in numerous letters whether money and other items he has sent have arrived safely. It is clear, however, that HSP was fortunate enough to receive all the mail his sons sent without charge: as he reminds them in 1822, 'I can get your letters and papers free now as ever, as the Earl of Rosse is still a Postmaster General' (L7). The situation with his own letters is less clear, but to judge by the compendious packages he sent, his friendship with Rosse, and perhaps also his own position as Postmaster for Galway until 1826, allowed him to send mail either free or at a significantly reduced rate. (Certainly, after 1826 those of his surviving letters which are complete are significantly shorter in length.) Internal evidence also shows that the letters were sent by whatever ship was most convenient, and whenever possible by merchant ships leaving from Galway harbour, rather than being routed through London for the official Post Office packet service to America. Here again, Persse's position as head figure in the Customs House suggests that he rarely had to pay regular mail costs, since he presumably needed to exert little influence to have his packages taken as a courtesy by the captains whose cargoes came under his scrutiny.[50] The unusually expansive quality of the correspondence, then, was the product of fortuitous circumstances, as well as of his personally liberal style.

IX

Henry Stratford Persse's letters present a classic portrait of the Old World looking fondly westward to the New. His vision of Ireland was incisive but always sceptical, and though resigned to dying himself in 'this Island of Slaves', he seems never to have surrendered the elasticity and resilience of mind that characterise even the most angry and despairing of his letters. Appropriately, the final surviving item of his correspondence, a fragment dating from late 1832 when he was in his early sixties, and written just a year before his death, shows him as animated as ever, enjoying the sensuous parlour fashions in vogue from Europe, and urging the pursuit of liberty with undiminished vigour:

> I am sure if Mr. Edwards could see his Daughters thus engaged that he would burn the mill and roar out 'Free Trade and the Graces for

ever' and for the future take his fabrics and fashions from Europe. Then the evenings could be spent with the Piano, and with Waltzing finish the night — when all might sing that 'love was Liberty and Natural Law'. (L22)

He died in October 1833. Of all his children left in Ireland, only one was settled properly, his daughter Matilda, who rather typically was married off to her first cousin, the wealthy Burton Persse of Moyode Castle. HSP had sold his interest in the Nuns' Island distillery at some point in the 1820s, and a year before his death Burton Persse assumed sole control of the business.[51] His other property seems to have likewise been assumed, either by bequest or by purchase, by other branches of the family. Lady Gregory, who seems never to have mentioned her great-uncle, and perhaps never heard of him, would herself spend childhood holidays at Newcastle House in the 1860s. Whatever papers were left at his death to mark his energetic record as businessman and independent thinker seem not to have survived for long, and only a few deeds held by University College, Galway, together with a few ruins and largely derelict buildings survive to attest to brewery and grain mill, although the solidly built distillery on Nuns' Island still stands and is currently being renovated as housing. His grave has not so far been located.

The Future

In your own hands are therefore your own fate. (L9, March 1823)

I

Dudley, Richard and Theophilus Persse did not debark from their ship at Boston in the autmn of 1821 without resources or plans well made beforehand. Apprenticeships had been arranged, letters of introduction written and sealed, and seed money provided with the promise of more to come from their hopeful father. Even so, the new environment they found, especially as they travelled down to New York City, must have overwhelmed them with its variety of opportunity. New York, in particular — both city and state — stood on the verge of explosive economic growth. Wealth, prosperity and 'immortality' were all predicted, with the fabled Erie Canal, begun just four years previously, at the heart of the splendid vision expected to materialise.[52] 'Great cities', wrote DeWitt Clinton in 1816, 'are universally created by commerce', and as merchants, investors, politicians, speculators and adventurers along the colonial eastern seaboard cast about for the means of enlarging the fortunes of Boston, New York, Philadelphia and Baltimore, all eyes turned west to the frontier that lay beyond the Appalachian chain.[53] In this single respect the city of New York, with its superb harbour and the Hudson River stretching far to the north, seemed perfectly positioned. Just 160 miles upstream lay the Mohawk River Valley, a natural intersect that cut a path westward through the mountains, connecting with inland lakes and other rivers to make a final thrust to Lakes Ontario and Erie, beyond which lay the treasures of seemingly limitless land and resources.

The value of the Mohawk had long been recognised, and control of the valley had long been fought over. Dutch, French, British and then American ambitions had targeted the region for well over a hundred years, even though its many sets of rapids, low water levels, shifting sand bars and difficult portages made commerce arduous and expensive. For all practical purposes, the river was largely unnavigable, and most western produce was conveyed by ox-drawn wagons over roads that often degenerated into long troughs of mud. In 1814 Robert Fulton calculated that the haulage of a single barrel of flour cost $2 to travel a single stretch of 130 miles, whereas from Albany to New York City by barge down the Hudson, a comparable distance, the cost was a mere 25 cents.[54] The economic benefits of developing the Mohawk seemed self-evident, however impractical the various schemes and projects that many entrepreneurs, such as Christopher Cowles of Ireland, previously employed on the River Shannon works, put forward. But as Thomas

Jefferson remarked, to connect New York City with the Great Lakes seemed premature, an idea that could not be achieved in the course of the nineteenth century. Yet Gouverneur Morris, standing on the shores of Lake Erie looking west, chaffed at delay: 'The proudest empire in Europe is but a bauble compared to what America *will* be, *must* be . . . As yet, my friend, we crawl along the outer shell of the country.'[55] Certainly the aura of New York was one of 'manifest destiny'. Between 1790 and 1820 the city's population tripled, and by the Civil War era it had far outstripped its principal rival, Philadelphia, in every commercial and demographic statistic then taken. In the year the Persse brothers landed in America only 8,000 immigrants from various European countries debarked via New York. A mere five years later the figure stood at 30,000, and a decade after that, 63,000. By 1852 the annual level of immigration in New York would climb to over 300,000, and many of these new arrivals headed west by way of the Erie Canal.[56]

Such was the optimistic drive of many in New York who were active in governmental and mercantile affairs, that even the staggering cost of $5 million to construct a canal from Albany on the Hudson to Buffalo on Lake Erie seemed eminently reasonable, despite the fact that in 1810, the year in which its legislature first voted to examine a feasible route and assemble projected costs, the entire revenue of New York State was only $626,000 per year.[57] The federal government was sufficiently daunted, both on financial and constitutional grounds, to shy away from involvement, and even many in the general populace were aghast. As one 'plain farmer' put it, 'Why should I be taxed to effect a plan which places the farmer at the head of Lake Michigan in a better situation than myself?'[58] But proponents of 'the Great Ditch', such as DeWitt Clinton, pleaded otherwise: 'I have seen some profound politicians, some cautious calculating men, speak of the projected canal as a great and desirable measure. But this, as they observe, is not the period for executing the work. The country is too young. There was not, in ancient mythology, a more instructive image than the figure of OPPORTUNITY. It had much hair on the forehead, but was bald behind — *Let the occasion pass, and you find nothing by which you can take hold of it* — A most critical and decisive period is at hand. If you sleep the tide, you may sleep forever.'[59]

II

No figure is more indelibly connected with the Erie Canal than DeWitt Clinton, whose extraordinary career exactly coincides with America's great turn to the west. Born in 1769 at New Britain, a small Hudson River village, Clinton began life with considerable advantages. His father's branch of the Clintons, having unsuccessfully followed the fortunes of King Charles I in England over a century before, had suffered confiscation and exile in the Stuart cause, wanderings that saw them uprooted through France, Spain, Scotland and Ulster until 1729, when DeWitt's grandfather, Charles, landed in America, eventually settling in New York. The Revolutionary War saw Clintons serving in both armies, the best known being Major-General Sir Henry Clinton, commander-in-chief of all British forces from the battle of Saratoga until 1782. DeWitt's father, James, and his uncle, George, Brigadier-Generals both in the Continental Army, each by coincidence lost engagements to Sir Henry, but when the regiments of Lord Cornwallis marched out of Yorktown to surrender in 1782, they filed past James, by now a distinguished and much travelled soldier, in command of his New York Brigade.

DeWitt Clinton received the first post-war diploma of the newly named Columbia University in 1784, entering the practice of law before serving his uncle George, now Governor of New York (and one day, a Vice-President), as private secretary for five years until 1795. Thus was launched a long, distinguished and controversial political career which saw him serve as a New York State Assemblyman and then Senator, three times Mayor of New York City, a United States Senator, Lieutenant Governor of New York, and three terms as Governor. In 1812 he was nominated for President by New York Republicans and Federalists from New England who opposed war with England, a conflict that the incumbent President James Madison, preaching 'righteous belligerancy', pursued under goading from those seeking new lands for settlement in Canada and the western frontier at British expense. Clinton won 89 electoral votes, carrying all the north-east except Vermont and Pennsylvania, but Madison swept every other state to win with 128.[60]

Beginning in 1810, and serving intermittently for the remainder of his life, Clinton laboured on the Erie Canal Commission as it first plotted the course, then campaigned for legislative approval, and finally raised the capital to begin work. These were exhausting years for Clinton, with much time spent on horseback, in stage-coaches, along mean country roads up and down the countryside, and passing from one wilderness village to another, all the while checking surveys, manipulating public opinion, giving speeches, and writing 'memorials' and pamphlets. Periods of optimism and incessant belief in the absolute necessity for a navigable waterway to connect the markets of New York with Ohio, Michigan, Indiana and Illinois alternated with terrible bouts of depression and doubt, particularly as funding mechanisms dried up or, after initial enthusiasm, simply backed away. His governmental experience proved indispensable when, as a last resort, the state of New York began debate on whether it should itself subsidise the construction through the issue of bonds. The financial commitment, undertaken as a result of Clinton's intensive lobbying, was so immense that it amounted to 33 per cent of New York's available inventory of banking and insurance capital.[61] In 1817 the first offering was made, and largely through purchases by individual small investors and one or two savings banks the entire run of bonds sold out, a subscription that would eventually total twenty-four seperate loans amounting to $7,411,770. On 4 July 1817 the first spadeful of earth was turned and work on 'Clinton's Ditch' — less charitably called 'Clinton's Folly' — was begun.

III

'Canallers!' cried Don Pedro . . . 'Who and what are they?'
'Canallers, Don, are the boatmen belonging to our Grand Erie Canal. You must have heard of it . . . For three hundred and sixty

miles, gentlemen, through the entire breath of the State of New York; through numerous populous cities and most thriving villages; through long, dismal, uninhabited swamps, and affluent, cultivated fields, unrivalled for fertility; by billiard-room and bar-room; through great forests; on Roman arches over Indian rivers; through sun and shade; by happy hearts or broken; through all the wide contrasting scenery of those noble Mohawk counties; and especially, by rows of snow-white chapels, whose spires stand almost like milestones, flows one continual stream.'

Herman Melville, *Moby Dick* (1851)[62]

One can scarcely imagine, driving through the economically depressed areas of upper New York State today, and passing occasionally an abandoned and derelict lock from the old Erie Canal, that here in the 1820s lay stretched one of the engineering miracles of pre-industrial times, what the poet Philip Freneau called 'a work from nature's *chaos* won',[63] and by another admirer 'a golden chord, a bind, in our national existence'.[64] For unlike the aqueducts of Rome, very little of 'The Big Ditch' survives today, the locks torn away to make way for roads, highways or parking lots, the 'basins' or artificial harbours used as municipal dumps or receptacles for derelict cars, the old tow-paths overgrown. In some places a twentieth-century barge canal, now too all but obsolete, supersedes its more primitive ancestor. At the time of its construction such images would have horrified those who laboured on the Erie. Their creation, it was expected, would last for ever.

That the canal was ever completed is remarkable. In 1817 the only engineering project in America involving hydraulics and sophisticated canal-building techniques was the relatively modest Middlesex system of 27 miles length that connected the Merrimack River with Boston Harbour. The Erie, by contrast, would run 363 miles, employ eighty-three locks, eighteen aqueducts (praised by the Marquis de Lafayette's secretary for their 'boldness of execution'), and raise a barge from the level of the Hudson 565 feet to that of Lake Erie.[65] Technological innovations ranging from land-clearing machinery to cement that hardened underwater and to the Du Pont Company's newest blend of blasting powder would all be developed and applied in almost casual fashion by men who had virtually no first-hand experience in monumental construction. Most of the head engineers, for example, had few mechanical skills other than the rudimentary aptitude for surveying. Yet in the summers of 1818 and 1819 they assembled, directed, cajoled and prodded a workforce that eventually totalled 9,000 men to dig and line a canal forty feet wide by four feet deep, supported in turn by maintenance systems of holding ponds, dams, feeders, levies and assorted engineering paraphernalia, all completed in the relatively modest span of eight years. When Governor DeWitt Clinton ceremoniously rode the first barge from the Erie to New York City on 4 November 1825, the *Seneca Chief* loaded with fertiliser, fish, flour, butter, wood and two kegs of water from the Great Lakes, he was greeted by a flotilla which signalled: 'Where bound?' Clinton had boatmen yell in reply: 'To the Atlantic!'

If festivities surrounding the canal's opening were spectacular, so too were the financial results announced by Clinton after one year of operation. The Erie, he declared, had generated over \$1,000,000 in tolls and other revenue, an unforeseen rate of return that would easily service the debt expenses of \$400,000 per annum.[66] The trade benefits were equally striking. Western goods coming east had totalled over 300,000 tons, and booming overseas trade in wheat, flower, salt and numerous other commodities flooded through New York City. Villages and former crossroads in upper New York State — Utica, Rome, Syracuse, Rochester, Lockport and Buffalo — began periods of unprecedented growth, as did many hitherto unknown trading posts on the Great Lakes such as Cleveland and Chicago. 'I look forward to a period', Clinton had written in 1816, 'in which every part of that wilderness will be divided into farms, and settled with industrious yeomanry.'[67] A mere decade later his predictions seemed eminently within reach.

IV

The Erie Canal, with its slow and ponderous travel, nonetheless attracted the attention of many Americans seeking to experience what was for them a new and unique experience. Melville, Mark Twain, William Dean Howells and Nathaniel Hawthorne, among others, all included descriptions of the Erie in their various works, Hawthorne's perhaps being the most risqué, as he described female passengers disrobing for bed in the very crowded passenger packets that soon plied the canal. 'The unquietness of my mind', he wrote, 'was relieved by a turn in the night air above deck.'[68] Howells pictured the countryside through which the Erie passed: 'its mild beauty and tranquil picturesqueness . . . everywhere generous slopes and pleasant hollows and the wide meadows of a grazing country, with the pretty brown Mohawk River rippling down through all'.[69] He neglected to mention how valuable all this property had suddenly become.

Much of the manoeuvring and planning for the Erie's route west, of course, had been dictated to some degree by the various commissioners' speculations and purchases of lands regarded hitherto as relatively worthless. George Washington, in partnership with George Clinton, had reaped windfall profits with lands along the Mohawk.[70] Even DeWitt Clinton was accused of illegal profiteering, though whatever gains he may have made did not seem unduly avaricious to most observers, since he had promised publicly, as part of his promotional activity on behalf of the canal, 'a vast increase in the value of lands, and a similar increase in wealth'.[71] The three Persse boys, freshly arrived in America, turned their eyes in the same direction as everyone else, towards the Mohawk River and the new riches it promised.

At the outset all three were apprenticed to farmers in the vicinity of Johnstown, New York, an agricultural community just four miles north of the Mohawk River and the Erie's proposed route from Amsterdam to Utica. The choice of this particular area was almost certainly determined by several factors: family communication with relatives in America; scattered pieces of economic forecasting and informed guesswork gleaned from English and Irish newspapers, which regularly reported on the canal; and, probably most influential of all, Henry Stratford's characteristically progressive notions as to the benefits such a project might deliver to those determined enough to profit by them.

The boys' maternal uncle, Clement Sadleir Sr, had resided in the United States since well before the turn of the nineteenth century. What drew him to the relatively undeveloped frontier west of Albany is not known, but his choice of Johnstown almost certainly owed to the fabled success of its founder, Sir William Johnson (1715–74), known throughout the British Isles for his wildly romantic efforts to create a semi-feudal barony in lands still roamed by the Six Nations, an Indian confederacy of Iroquois tribes. Johnson, the progeny of minor gentry from Smithstown, County Meath, had been lured to the Americas by his own uncle, Admiral Sir Peter Warren, renowned for his command of naval forces at the storming of Louisbourg in Cape Breton and, most particularly, his glorious victory over the French Admiral La Jonquiere off the Spanish coast in May 1747. Wealthy through generous rewards from a grateful parliament and his many privateering exploits (£127,000 in prize money alone), Sir Peter owned two palatial homes on Manhattan island, a city residence on what is now lower Broadway, and a country seat of 300 acres that he called Greenwich Hall, the site of today's Greenwich Village, from where he married into one of the premier merchant families of Dutch New York, the De Lanceys. Through their machinations Warren came into possession of 14,000 acres of Mohawk Valley real estate for the sum of £110, and to his nephew William he gave the position of land agent.[72]

Once on site, however, Johnson immediately fell victim to the entrepreneurial spirit common to most frontiers. Admiring of and open to Indian ways, he soon gained the confidence of Iroquois fur traders and chieftains, learning their language and customs, going native in dress and habit, cohabiting with their women and allegedly siring many offspring, all the time acquiring land on his own and making considerable sums through trade with soldiers, settlers and aborigines alike. During three wars he proved his mettle as a leader of irregular forces, however

galling the demeanour that he and his Indians presented to the aristo-
cratic likes of Lord Jeffrey Amherst and other British officers, and he
emerged from these conflicts beweighted with titles and grants. For
eleven years, after building his manor house Johnson Hall in 1763, Sir
William conducted his affairs in much the same fashion as a palatine
lord of the marches. His enormous estates, to which he lured hundreds
of settlers, many from his native country, were developed along the
lines of Anglo-Norman swordland. The demesne surrounding Johnson
Hall featured a 500-acre park, ornamental gardens, dairy, forge, stable,
a whole array of domestic services, and even a lake complete with a
crannóg. He built schools, churches, courthouses, forts and prisons,
served as merchant, negotiator, soldier, defender, Indian administrator,
farmer and judge as times or circumstances warranted, all the while
smoking peace-pipes, joining his blind Irish piper in song, performing
a minuet or war-dance depending on the occasion, and generally amass-
ing a body of heroic saga unrivalled by any single figure in the colonies.
Coffee-houses in London reeled with the gossip of his adventures, both
military and amorous, and the Limerick-born writer Charles Johnstone
highlighted his career in the novel *Chrysal, or The Adventures of a Guinea*,
portraying Johnson as a figure of almost biblical mystique followed
around by a harem of compliant squaws.[73] Johnstown, named after its
benefactor in 1771, was known far and wide in the British Isles, especially after the American War of Independence when the sudden collapse of this loyalist family made for instructive and melodramatic
reading.[74]

Clement Sadleir made no such mistake of judgement in 1812 when
Great Britain again went to war with its former colonies. Sadleir by
then was a respected lawyer in Johnstown. He had served as the principal justice of the town since 1810, and his son did not hesitate to volunteer for service when hostilities began, suffering major wounds as a
captain of American infantry at Little York, Upper Canada, in April
1813. When Henry Stratford Persse determined to send his boys
abroad, he turned for advice to his brother-in-law, who certainly
informed him that the economic barometer of Johnstown was now as

buoyant as at any time since Sir William's fame and fortune, and that the Erie had become everyone's focus.

Henry Stratford Persse refers twice in his letters to the study of maps involving the canal and its proposed routes through upper New York State. 'A very superior present,' he notes on 16 February 1822 of one sent home by the boys. 'I have it hung in the drawing room and Mr. Morris and I have travelled from New York to Johnstown a hundred times and often on to Lake Erie by the Canal.' More informational were press reports on the canal's progress that appeared in English newspapers, particularly *The Gentleman's Magazine* and *The Times* of London, all reflecting the growing interest of Europeans in America's progress.[75] One irony involving the Erie was the sudden and fairly dramatic increase of foreign investment, particularly from Great Britain. An important rationale for the canal's construction had been American awareness of transportation difficulties during the war of 1812. Anticipating further conflict with England over Canada's dominion, backers of the canal argued that quick movement of cannon and supplies up-country to the battlefront alone justified its expense. Yet after the relatively quick and scandal-free repayment of the first bond issue, it was English financial resources that made future offerings easier to sell. 'All rich men are timid,' a merchant once told Clinton; but after 1822 over a third of all investment in the canal came from just the country its creation was meant to stymie.[76] The talk on Galway's streets may have supplied additional details of the opportunity the area provided. As the largest public works project ever initiated in North America, word of employment and development opportunities inevitably filtered back to the old country, whether through returning Irishmen, papers and magazines, or ballads. A song of the times, 'Paddy on the Canal', confirms that the Erie was a magnet for many aspiring emigrants.[77]

V

Persse's correspondence with Clinton, a series of at least five letters beginning in April 1821 and continuing through August 1824, is a curious blend of sycophancy and quirky independence, obsequiousness and near incivility. His initial motivations in beginning the correspondence seem to have embodied a compound of impulses: a genuine admiration for the man behind the Erie, that 'gigantic enterprise' (L11) he hoped would benefit his sons; the wish to emulate his father's exchange of letters with a famous American; the hope that his practical experiences with the 'musty traditions' of bankrupt Europe would benefit the rulers of the fresh new land he idealised (L11); and, despite his protestations to the contrary, the blatant desire to introduce his three boys to someone who could further their interests. The Governor's replies, like Washington's to William Persse, were formal and polite, and usually accompanied by Clinton's latest pamphlet on the Erie.[78] Whether any of Persse's sons actually gained advancement from introduction to Clinton — and there is evidence that they did indeed meet — is not known.

The principal matter of expertise that Persse sought to exchange with the Governor involved his lifetime of work at the Customs House in Galway city — the day-to-day knowledge of collections and duties, tariffs and ledgers, and the operation of waterways. His letter of 9 April 1821, not published in this volume, is a brief memo on the debilitating blights of patronage and bureaucracy, factors that Persse estimated were draining the fortunes of the Grand Canal in Ireland to the extent of an astonishing 45 per cent of revenues. That dated 4 June 1824, a far more interesting document, includes an astonishing harangue on the necessity of tariff protection for American manufacturers. The intemperate and highly emotional character of this letter may be in part attributable to an accident HSP had suffered to his arm. By necessity he dictated the letter to yet another of his sons, giving the narrative a distinctive rising rhythm as he warmed to the subject at hand. The tone is charged with personal intensity; and in sharp contrast to the fawning manner in his other letters to Clinton, Persse argues passionately, letting diplomatic caution fly to the winds. No less an issue than America's choice between real freedom and economic dependence lay behind his outburst. What George Washington and DeWitt Clinton had respectively won on the battlefield and through the great commercial enterprise of the Erie Canal stood to be squandered if the young republic failed to confront the economic challenges that Great Britain, 'this sleeping lion', and feudal Europe now posed. Their greatest desire, in Persse's opinion, was 'to gather strength, to destroy you'.

Before 1800 the question of protection had largely been academic, there being no significant American industry to support. The former colonies had been exploited for their raw materials and, in return, imported their finished goods from abroad. The modest tariffs that Congress occasionally authorised were justified as revenue producers, enabling the federal government to operate without direct taxation of its citizenry. Despite Alexander Hamilton's ambitious *Report of Manufacturers* (1789), which argued eloquently for the spark a tariff wall would provide to native production, Adam Smith's *The Wealth of Nations*, published in Philadelphia that same year, spoke more convincingly to the ideals of unhindered and open competition, a notion more inherently congenial to the ambitious and optimistic mindset of American entrepreneurs.

The Federalist position throughout the war of 1812 had been the cry of free trade. The great merchants of Boston and New York, the lesser traders of Rhode Island and Connecticut, Maine and New Jersey, all viewed the interruption of commerce by any means as a direct threat to life and happiness. Jefferson's Embargo Act, and Madison's ruinous choice of Great Britain as an opponent in war rather than the duplicitous Napoleon, were both deemed detrimental to the maritime interests of New England. The fact that belligerence towards Britain temporarily benefited the coffers of banks and merchant houses all along the eastern coast of America did not stop the Federalists from denouncing it.

With trade disrupted, American manufacturing, still in its infancy, sought to produce necessities for its own domestic market, and the north-east began its transition from a trading economy based on coastal centres to an inland industrial economy centred on water power and mills. The shift was so subtle that most observers barely realised what was happening. Federalist politicians continued preaching free trade and no tariffs at the same time that their regional economies required just the opposite. Eight thousand mechanised spinners in the cotton and linen trades in 1807 grew tenfold by 1810 to 80,000, and by 1812 the number had bounded to half a million, mostly in Rhode Island and Massachusetts.[79] But mill-owners panicked when normalisation of economic ties with Britain led to the American market being flooded with cheaper British goods. Import levels jumped from $13 million to $113 million in just six months after peace was declared in December 1814, and rose to $146 million by 1816. Sectional and competing commercial interests cracked apart the usual party lines of Federalists and Jeffersonians, and the heated debate over tariffs that ensued saw many unlikely alliances formed and more than a few longstanding friendships sundered.[80]

For DeWitt Clinton, the stakes were enormous. Like his uncle before him, Clinton affected Republican sympathies through most of his career. It had been an ironic moment when he had won the backing of regional Federalists during his unsuccessful campaign for the presidency in 1812. Unlike Jefferson, though, he was committed to an activist government, and especially to schemes, such as the Erie Canal, which dwarfed the enterprises that individuals were able to undertake. He had not hesitated to lobby for federal aid to support that venture and, when rebuffed, had unflinchingly manoeuvred his own state to fund it, despite the enormous political and economic risks involved. During his third term as Governor of New York, however, he opposed efforts by Federalist bureaucrats to collect duties on the canal, adopting a state rights position that would be heard again and again over the next forty years.[81] Simultaneously, and with considerable chagrin, he found his own power base, the merchants and traders of New York, almost universally in favour of a federally implemented tariff wall. Clinton, in the words of a contemporary, 'was sceptical of that policy which looked to the government for its interference and protection', but politically he hardly dared a provocative opposition.[82] His admirer in far-away Galway, primed either by his sons or, more likely, by reading the extensive reports of the tariff debate published in American and British newspapers, seems to have been closely acquainted with Clinton's wavering stance, and his long and emotional argument for the tariff was the result.

Drawing on local examples, Persse detailed how his own country was 'miserable beyond expression', gutted by taxes paid to an England that stripped it of every resource and offered nothing in return. America, by contrast, had the opportunity to develop a manufacturing base so strong that it would be placed 'beyond the reach of [European] ambition and despotism' (L11). America did not need cloth from Britain or iron from Sweden: she could develop her own resources to the benefit of her own, and become as mighty a commercial power as 'Old England' had ever been. 'Nations, like individuals, must make sacrifices. America must serve her apprenticeship to manufactures,' he argued, 'and while her sons are in a state of probation, they must be protected.' Otherwise, the '*canaille* of Europe' would flood American markets with the produce of their slave labour, and the new country would soon find itself commercially chained to 'the old and tottering *regime*' (L11). HSP's point of view was in fact virtually identical to those held by Senators John Calhoun of South Carolina and Henry Clay of Kentucky. Clay had coined the famous phrase 'The American System': namely, tariff protection enacted hand in hand with the development of a transportation network — chiefly turnpikes and canals — that could bring raw materials, resultant manufactured products and markets of people together in one interlocking, harmonious whole. Such a scheme was utopia to a man like Persse. He recognised, as Thomas Jefferson finally had, that no nation could stand on its agricultural or its industrial base alone. The blending of the two was both desirable and essential.

By 1824 Clinton's position on the tariff had taken definitive shape. Though New York City's Chamber of Commerce (representing the interests of merchants and importers of foreign goods) issued a statement strongly denouncing protective duties, Clinton heeded both the advice of manufacturers and his own sense of pragmatic politics, the sort that had fuelled his enthusiasm for the Erie Canal, by becoming a strong advocate for the protective tariff wall, which subsequently passed the Senate by only four votes and the House of Representatives by five. According to the historian George Dangerfield, 'It was Clinton's fate, and in some measure his deserts, to be suspected of everything', and many of his opponents refused to attribute his decision to anything but self-interest. Even those who agreed with his decision proceeded to denigrate his character, with tariff champion John Calhoun commenting a year later that the Governor 'wants, I apprehend, both patriotism and sagacity'.[83]

VI

Of all the Persse boys, Theophilus alone settled permanently in the Johnstown area of upper New York State. His first purchase of land two years after his marriage to a local girl in 1829 was a substantial portion of an original colonial land grant known as Butler's Patent,[84] named after the local grantee, Colonel John Butler, an infamous Tory who savaged his own tenantry during the guerrilla warfare of the Revolution. HSP had advised his son on the suitable location for this proposed farmstead, favouring the river and canalside property of Fonda, New York, as opposed to the higher bluffs of Johnstown proper, four miles away. He also contributed substantially to the $700 sale price. This was to be only the first in a long series of farms owned by Theophilus and his descendants. Just as DeWitt Clinton had predicted, the farming economy of western New York changed considerably as the Erie Canal snaked westwards across the state to Lake Erie. In twenty-five-mile swathes on either side of it farmers adapted to the availability of new markets, often specialising in a single crop or single livestock that could be sold direct to New York City or other developing urban centres. No longer would agricultural workers be simply subsistence farmers or, in Clinton's words, 'scattered inhabitants of a wilderness . . . who have done little more than build shelters for their families and raise a little corn for their support'.[85] Land values soared, often to four or five times the price per acre of virgin western land.

What the Erie Canal began, the railroads finished. Theophilus's (and Henry Stratford's) judgement on the site of his farm proved spectacularly prescient when the Utica and Schenectady Railroad laid tracks alongside the canal in 1835. Fonda, a mere village, was suddenly outfitted with a railway hotel and other mercantile amenities from which Theophilus profited. Gradually he expanded his holdings and moved to Johnstown proper, becoming a gentleman farmer and merchant. The family dairy business that he began there flourished, continuing in operation until the 1960s. Various descendants still own substantial acreage in the vicinity. The railroads, though, eventually undermined the Erie Canal's viability. Canal tonnage and revenues continued briskly through the 1850s, but the Civil War and resulting expansion of rail grids throughout the country spelled disaster for older and slower modes of transport. Even the abolition of tolls and fees after the war could not stem its decline.[86]

The fortunes of the other Persse brothers varied widely. It appears that Richard never found his niche in the New World. Five years after his departure from Ireland his brother Dudley noted in a letter to Theophilus that Richard had returned home and was very poorly off indeed: 'Richard says that he is so much in want of clothes that he is ashamed to go anywhere. My Aunt Mary sent him a pound note from Cork and wanted him to come and see her which I believe he intends doing before he leaves the Island.'[87] HSP refers to Richard's inconvenient presence in three letters, and evidently urged him to try America again, wishing, when he did eventually take ship again, that 'poor Richard will now get on'. However, an intersibling letter of 1841, written from Ireland, shows that he had once again retreated to the environs of his birth, this time apparently for good.[88]

Dudley's career proved more colourful. Excitement kindled by the success of the Erie Canal encouraged the formation of many private companies seeking to replicate, on a smaller scale, the benefits it had allowed. The Connecticut River, for instance, beginning at the city of New Haven on Long Island Sound, was potentially navigable as far north as Barnet, Vermont. In 1829 the last set of inhibiting rapids was

bypassed by a five-and-a-half-mile canal constructed by the Connecticut River Corporation using 400 Irish labourers under the supervision
of an Erie veteran.[89] A new town sprang up known as Windsor Locks,
and up to eight steamers a day began plying the river between Spring-
field and Hartford, traffic described by the visiting Charles Dickens in
American Notes (1842).[90] As with the Erie, railroads eventually rendered
the Enfield Canal obsolete as a navigational necessity, but industry continued to settle along the waterway to utilise the works for power. Thirteen factories clustered along the canal by 1880, and in Hartford
County no fewer than twenty-five paper mills were in operation.[91]

Dudley Persse, after serving some eight years as apprentice and
clerk in various mercantile establishments, is recorded by his father as
entering into partnership with another merchant in 1829. By 1840 his
business interests had become quite substantial and along with his attorney, Horace Brooks, he opened an office on Nassau Street in New York,
engaging in the paper trade.[92] Two years later they purchased an existing mill at Windsor Locks and began the manufacture of book and bind-
ing papers, a business of considerable profitability for some ten years.
Among their better known accounts was the *New York Herald*, printed
on Persse & Brooks newsprint. In 1849 a friend of Theophilus's wife
wrote a letter to Johnstown describing Dudley's 'beautiful mansion' in
'the most improved part of Brooklyn', commenting approvingly that
'the grounds around [the house] are very tasty'.[93] By the early 1850s
business was so brisk that Dudley invited Theophilus to join the firm,
and when his younger brother did so he was given a position at the
Windsor Locks mill. In 1854, however, the Connecticut operation ran
into major difficulties and Dudley was forced into bankruptcy, which
included the humiliating inventory and auction of all his possessions
within that state ('1 sofa, $9; 1 mirror, $1.50; 1 dressing table, .50; 4
bedsteads, $3.00; 18 prs of sheets, $9', and so forth).[94] Taking advantage of the speculative mania then infecting all the major market-places
in the country, Persse & Brooks now gambled everything on a major
recapitalisation initiative, raising close to half a million dollars in stock
offering and bank notes. They then constructed in Windsor Locks what

many contemporaries called the largest and most efficient paper mill ever built in the United States, only to see their grandiloquent enterprise brought to ruin in the panic of 1857, when every bank in New York City save one was forced to close its doors in the face of investor runs.[95] Manufacturers such as Dudley, engulfed in debt, could not hope to repay their notes, and Persse & Brooks again declared bankruptcy, with claims against the company totalling $369,730 against assets of only $115,000.[96] One of Dudley's major competitors in the trade, C. W. Dexter, inventor of manila paper (the process of manufacturing heavy-duty wrap from the fibre of a Philippine tree), oversaw the dismemberment and auction of the famous mill.

From the wreckage of Dudley's business empire, Theophilus moved on to the management of a grocery store purchased in Windsor Locks and a brief career in politics, running for the state legislature in April 1860 as an anti-war Democrat. The newly formed Republican Party swept the local and federal elections of that year — 'A Glorious Result' exulted the *Hartford Courant* — but Theophilus and two Democratic colleagues from neighbouring Windsor managed to win their races in the face of Lincoln's popularity, doubtless due to the Irish and labouring composition of their constituencies.[97] 'Hurrah for Old Windsor!' wrote the otherwise chastened *Daily Times* of Hartford, a rabidly anti-Republican paper which habitually denounced the President's 'imbecility', printed reams of criticism of Wendell Phillips and other noted 'negro worshippers', and praised the South and its supporters in Congress.[98] Theophilus served, at $2.50 a day, for but one term only. He eventually retired to Johnstown, where he died on 13 December 1880.[99]

Theophilus lived long enough to see his own children establish themselves successfully in the mainstream of American life. His eldest son, named Henry Stratford Persse, born in 1838, flourished as an entrepreneur, eventually moving west to Colorado, where in his declining years he acquired a celebrated beauty-spot on the outskirts of the city of Denver, which he named 'Roxborough Park'. In an interview given to the Denver *Daily News* in 1911 he lists the many Persse heirlooms he had inherited, including letters sent to America by his grandmother

Anne, Henry Stratford's wife, soon after the voyage of 1821.[100] These and other items are currently untraced, but may still survive. Theophilus's third son, Theophilus Blakeney Persse, took over his father's grocery business, followed him into the Connecticut state legislature in 1874 (with similarly modest success) and married well by gaining the hand of the daughter of John Windsor of Windsor Locks.

Of HSP's other children, the record is mixed. His eighth son, Thomas Moore Persse, whom he sent out to join Dudley, Richard and Theophilus in 1829, soon returned to Ireland, where he parlayed both his American experience and also perhaps family connections to gain positions as a Landwaiter and US Consul in the port of Dublin. By 1841 he had returned to Galway, where he became proprietor of a distillery adjoining the property at Newcastle, formerly run by his brother-in-law, Burton Persse. When his lease on this property expired around 1847, he took over and restored the old Nuns' Island distillery his father had established.[101] *Thom's Directory* for 1852 lists him as serving as magistrate for the borough, barony cess-collector for Dunkellin, and US Consul (this last perhaps being merely an honorary title retained from his Dublin career). The 'lick plate' sons HSP had feared for, however, seem to have come to little good. William, stuck in the 'same way' as a thirty-six-year-old, according to HSP's letter of June 1828, died apparently unmarried and without recorded achievement. An 1841 letter from Thomas Moore Persse to Theophilus refers tolerantly to him in passing as 'the same good natured creature'.[102] Henry Persse died unmarried during the Galway cholera outbreak of 1832, while Robert Dudley Persse, his third son, enjoyed modest success in his career as a minor official in the Post Office. HSP's remaining three sons all emigrated to the USA, the two youngest (Frank and 'the weakest reed' (L16), Burton), doing so during HSP's last three years of life, and Parsons Persse at a date unknown. HSP's elder daughter, Sally, is recorded in these letters as having made a 'hasty match' to one Stephen Creagh (L17), in part perhaps since she was already in her thirties, and his final letter laments the 'great burthen' the couple had been to him since the marriage, and his hopes that they too would be able to emigrate.[103] His younger daughter, Mattie, bore at least three children to her cousin Burton Persse of Moyode, becoming in HSP's eyes 'as good a Mother and Wife as she was a Daughter or a Sister' (L22). It would be Mattie who took principal responsibility for her mother, Anne Persse, after HSP's death. Apparently left with little money, Anne Persse went to live at Moyode Castle, where she lived into her eighties. In a fragmentary letter dating to around 1852, probably to Theophilus, she reflects that 'I am now nearly nineteen years in Dudley's house' and praises her 'darling Mattie and her good natured husband' for their unfailing 'kindness and attention to me and mine'.[104] Mattie herself died aged seventy-three in 1862, leaving her brother Thomas Persse, who died in 1884, as the last of HSP's children to remain on Irish soil.

Editorial Note

Henry Stratford Persse's generously sized and smoothly flowing handwriting in the main proved easily legible. His punctuation and use of orthographic conventions such as paragraph breaks, however, were highly erratic. In order to present these letters in an easily readable form, we have regularised our transcriptions to accord more closely with modern usage by supplying commas, full stops and question marks where needed. We have also inserted paragraph breaks in a number of places, and replaced Persse's occasional use of dashes between sentences with the full stops that would now be expected. Abbreviations have been silently expanded throughout, and ampersands replaced with 'and'.

Persse's spelling was generally excellent. We have modernised a few now archaic forms, presenting 'packets' for 'packetts', for instance, and 'lots' for lotts', and have also joined some words he left separate, 'news papers' becoming 'newspapers', for instance, and 'any body' becoming 'anybody'. Place-names are given in their current form where identifiable. Occasional spelling mistakes in proper names are also silently corrected, unless the misspellings seem to signal a significant lack of knowledge (for instance in his error 'Tomkins' for Governor Tompkins of New York). In such cases we have supplied the missing letters within square brackets. Throughout, these square brackets signal the insertion of editorial material, except in cases where a question mark is present within the brackets, to signal an uncertain reading. In a few places the manuscripts are torn and text is missing; tears are represented with angled brackets, thus: < . . . >.

Persse's use of capitalisation was also erratic. We have preserved throughout his consistent use of capitalisation in phrases such as 'Dearest Boys', and in places where it seems clear that he wished to signal emphasis — such as in 'Farmers' or 'Landlords' — but have presented lower case in places where his capitalisations seem merely capricious. In all other respects, the essential features of his prose are presented as directly as possible.

For the sake of convenience and brevity, the initials HSP are frequently used in the Introduction and other editorial comment to denote the name Henry Stratford Persse.

Letters of Henry Stratford Persse to his Sons
1821–1832

Letter 1

[Dudley, Richard and Theophilus, the fifth, sixth and seventh of HSP's ten sons, sailed for New York on 4 August 1821. Dudley was aged approximately eighteen, with Theophilus, the youngest of the three, just fifteen. HSP had entrusted oversight of their financial arrangements to his brother-in-law Clement Sadleir, who he clearly hoped would stand in loco parentis to them in the New World, but his trust in the family connection was later to prove sadly misplaced. This first letter makes a characteristic request for information about economic and social conditions in the United States and reflects HSP's underlying anxiety as to whether he has indeed done the right thing by encouraging his sons to emigrate.]

Galway Octob<er> [1821]

My Dear Theophilus,

On Saturday we received your letter dated the 3rd of September last from New York, and you can form no idea [of] the happiness we all felt at hearing of your safe arrival and also that Mr Sadleir had received you so kindly. Your poor Mother, though she would not admit to Mrs Shone that she was glad, was quite pleased with your Uncle's letter and says now that he was always the best natured of her Father's family. She says now I was right in sending you all out, and that I ought never to mind her but to take my own way in what I think the best for you.

I must hope when I hear again from you that you will give me an account of the condition of the people compared with that of the working and industrious classes in this country, for I long to learn from you and the Boys the appearance, the food, the clothing and housing of the American People, for we are told in the English papers that the United States swarm with beggars and that the Farmers and Tradespeople are starving. In future, take a week or two to write a letter, a few lines every day, when any thought occurs to you or any circumstance awakens your recollection, and by this means you will be able without much trouble to yourself

[pages missing]

but are < . . . > the weather is the worst <I ever?> knew in Ireland, <it never?> ceases raining at all, and <we?> had slight snow yesterday.

So many have taken up the pen to write to you that they only leave me to say that I am, with love to the Boys, whom I praise God are arrived, and regards to all your Cousins,

my Dear Theophilus,

your ever fond and affectionate Father,

H. S. Persse

Letter 2

[From New York the Persse brothers made a 'roundabout voyage' via Boston to Johnstown, in upper New York State, where they were to enter into a term of employment as labourer-apprentices on a farm. HSP here recalls the part played in the American War of Independence by his uncle Colonel William Blakeney (1735–1804), who had fought with the Welsh Fusiliers. Blakeney was a brother of HSP's mother, Sarah Blakeney Persse (d. 1792). HSP's 'Aunt Betty' was Elizabeth Persse Lambert, who had married Walter Lambert (d. 1824) of Castle Lambert, County Galway, in 1791. No record of the journals HSP evidently encouraged his sons to keep during their voyage seems to have survived.]

Galway

December 21 1821

My Darling Boys,

I am so overjoyed at hearing of your safe arrival at Boston (a Yankee town), that I know not how better to commence my letter to you than by returning the Almighty God thanks for the protection afforded you over the perilous deep, and I pray most fervently to Heaven to bless and foster any desire of yours that tends to your own happiness, so long as you put your trust in Him and such happiness tends not to the injury of your neighbour.

I suppose at Boston you saw Bunkers Hill, where your Great-Uncle Col. William Blakeney of the 17th Regiment was shot in the breast, and though the ball was never extracted, he lived *many* years afterwards. He told me, on that day says he 'all the men of my Company were nearly killed or wounded. One man from the County of Galway who always stepped out with the *wrong* foot was near me. He asked me

[*twenty manuscript pages missing*]

sprung from the very fibres of my Heart, and let me hear that although you may be *poor* in purse you are *rich* in *Character* and *conduct*. I am not forgetful of your wants. I know what you lost by your roundabout voyage, and I promise you I shall soon have that loss repaid you, but just at this moment I am pressed. I hope I shall soon hear from each, with the particulars of a copy from the *Journal* each of you kept of his voyage, what he saw and the remarks he made —

I send you lots of newspapers, and I write to my Aunt Betty to Cork to send you a present of potatoes to give to your friends.

All this house join me in love to you three, to your Uncle, Cousins and all their family, and believe me to ever remain my Excellent Boys,

your ever fond and affectionate Father
Henry S. Persse

When each is settled in his own abode I shall write seperately to each, but now write to all together.

Letter 3

[*This letter follows on immediately from the closure of HSP's last, but not yet having heard again from his sons, he now begins to turn his attention to his own news and news of the country they had left.*

The heavy rains occurring in the winter of 1821–22, which caused severe crop damage, ushered in a period of extreme social and economic crisis in Ireland. Agrarian unrest had been building up for some time as a result of the sharp fall in corn prices since 1816, new taxes levied following the amalgamation of the Irish and English exchequers in 1817, and an earlier episode of crop failure in 1816 that had been followed by a devastating outbreak of typhus fever. By the summer of 1822 scattered violence had given way to widespread large-scale insurrection in parts of County Cork, while in Connacht much of the population faced the prospect of starvation. The government set up relief projects such as road-building, which provided the only means of survival for nearly a million people in Connacht at the height of the crisis, but the continuing supremacy of laissez-faire politics ensured that such schemes were less comprehensive than was required. Symptomatically, the government's principal response was to reintroduce the Insurrection Act in February 1822, legislation that had already been in force between 1814 and 1818. The act allowed the imposition of curfews and the suspension of trial by jury in areas of unrest, and led to the brief phase of 'human carnage' HSP describes bitterly below.

HSP had entered into correspondence with DeWitt Clinton (1769–1828), the major figure in New York politics of the era, beginning in April 1821, a move which reflected both the strength of his interest in political and social conditions in America and, despite his protestations to the contrary, his intent to further his sons' prospects. He continued to correspond with Clinton (who served as Mayor of New York for all but two years between 1803 and 1815, and as Governor of New York 1817–23 and 1825–28) at least until 1825, expressing his views on such topics as tariffs and taxation. Clinton, and his predecessor as Governor, Daniel D. Tompkins (1774–1825) — who was Vice-President from 1817 to 1825 — were liberal reformers of the kind HSP could readily admire. Tompkins had legislated the ending of slavery in New York State during his term of office.

HSP mentions both of his daughters, Sally and Matilda ('Mattie', b. 1789) in this letter, along with his four eldest 'lick plate' sons: William, Henry (b. c. 1795), Robert and Parsons. Parsons later followed Dudley, Richard and Theophilus to America, as did 'Tommy' Persse, HSP's eighth son, who emigrated in 1824.]

Galway
February 16 1822

My Dear Boys,

Having just finished my Packet, which I sent you by a vessel from Dublin with 9 gold sovereigns enclosed in it, I now begin anew, and I continue to address you *conjointly*, that is all together, until I find that you are fixed each at his own destination.

My last letter ended in Wet, Wet, Wet, and here we have still the same weather, no stirring out, and fuel so scarce and dear that the poor perish with cold and wet, and the rich are straightened [*straitened*] to pay the additional expense that the high price of fuel imposes on them. Nothing but dire necessity keeps me tied to this Island, for so filthy a climate the world cannot produce.

I now enclose you copies of two letters I received from your Governor, De Witt Clinton, and in making him known to you, I think it right to inform you that did I imagine that my making you acquainted with this distinguished and most excellent man was to kindle in your minds a hope that through his influence you were to advance yourselves without the aid of your industry I should decline the introduction altogether. But I hope you are above the mean idea in a free country, and that you have that just and independent pride about you that revolts at the thought of living upon the labours of others. Thank Heaven! it is wisely ordained in America that the Governor (or Lord Lieutenant as we should call him) has not the power to grind down millions of Human Beings for the purpose of fattening and corrupting a few worthless sycophants. No! God be praised! He has not, and every day's experience will blessedly unfold to you that in the Country of your adoption, nothing is set down to *Name* or *Condition* and that every man is estimated by his net value, and by no other standard. In *this* country you know that the most ignorant, if they possess interest, are elevated to the highest places, but as I often told you, with you 'Merit Makes the Man' and is the only high road to rewards. I believe Governor Tom[p]kins who preceeded Clinton was but the son of a Farmer. The father is still I imagine alive and is not ashamed to drive his wagon to market. And surely you cannot admire that policy which would (had I been born before your Uncle Robert)[1] have given all the family estates to William and treat all my other sons as if they were bastards, and my eldest *only* as a legitimate. When therefore you shall be introduced to the Governor you must only consider yourselves introduced to a highly respectable country gentleman, of very rare and transcendent abilities, from whom you may receive much civility, but to whom you are not to look to for any favours, as he has not the power to rob the many to enrich a few. I hope therefore, my Dearest Boys, that you will seek always to learn the road to independence and having attained it that you will proudly reflect that you hold in your own person the means of preferment and that you are not dependent on the caprice or the whim of any man, and that while others lose their lives in *expectancy*, *you* build your promotion upon the certain rock of your own capability.

The accounts from Limerick and Cork are beyond any description. No man's life is there safe. It is a regular war between the oppressors and the oppressed, and in this scene of human carnage, I dare say you would not wish to earn a laurel at *either* side. In Mrs. Connolly's paper (she writing with an muffled pen) compares this war to the insurrection of the Blacks and calls Ireland a second Hispaniola or St. Domingo and it is true, for there human beings were put to death like wild beasts while the conflict lasted between the slaves and the slave owners. But since man obtained his just rights there, all is quietness and peace[2] —

Febuary 20 — Mr. Dillon of New York is just come here. He brought me the map which I look upon as a very superior present. I have it hung in the drawing room and Mr. Morris and I have travelled from New York to Johnstown a hundred times and as often on to Lake Erie by the Canal. This and the book the Governor sent me makes me quite at home. I also got some newspapers but not one that I would give a rush for, the Mercantile Advertizements and Ship Lists in the *New York Evening Post* and the *New York Gazette and General Advertizer* are worth near nothing. It *is reading I want*, and they contain none.

I did not get from Mr. Dillon the Governor's Speech. He did not get it he said, but I got it from another, and I am delighted with it. I like the accounts of the 4th [of] July and I like very much the accounts of the Cattle Shows and Farming Societies and Premiums and in all the papers sent me not a word of either to be seen.

I got Mr. Darby's tour.[3] He seems to me to be a romancer or novelist, some person sent out to draw sketches for landscape painters. His book is like a place in America called *Point no Point*. Though you are in full sail and see the Point still you never can round it.

As I heard that Mr. Dillon had paid attention to Theophilus, I asked him and Warden Ffrench to dinner. Your mother was quite pleased to see him but what was the wonder of the [Capenters?] when they heard that this chap that left this five years ago almost starving should dine with me, but when they saw his elegant dress they cried Wirra Sthru![4] in earnest and when he walks the street there are numbers pointing to him as the American Nabob.

Mr. Vandeleur is made a Judge of, and think how lucky John Lambert is to be his Register.[5] I hope he will be prudent as the Judge's is a very bad life, and if he trips off what must become of John and his pride. John Burke never wrote a line home to his wife or anybody else. They think he is dead.

[February] 25th — Sally is just returned from Castle Lambert. She was at Ballymore and Persse Lodge, Belville etc. and now poor Matty is gone to take a spell in the country air which she wanted. Robert we never hear a single word about. He is I believe at Castleboy. William is at Sir Richard St. George's.[6] He just sent me a nice greyhound bitch, but I would prefer *Hero* that is in Connemara. Little Captain Flaherty formerly of the John is going to Liverpool to buy a good large vessel. Pat Flaherty of Arran joins him. He intends to bring her here and take a whole colony from Arran in her in June next to Baltimore in America. I wish he would go to New York and I could send many things by her to you, but I yet hope a vessel may come here from New York or Philadelphia, as flax seed is so cheap this year.

John O'Flynn and Ward are in jail for shooting without a licence. Will your neighbours believe this, there are letters from America in town dated 6 weeks later than yours. You know we are anxious to hear of you and from you, but I know we cannot hear satisfactorily from you till next November or December when you will have seen the country in all its seasons, and be able to speak from absolute experience. Matty is at Castle Lambert, and Sally now at home. We have had a week of tolerable dry weather, but it is all rain and storm again. A boat from Arran

I see wrecked at Seaview, people saved at Fort Hill. William who you know is a great person for getting people places has got Madgy to be cook at Sir Richard St. George's.

Poor Coffee and wife and children are still here unprovided for. I fear they will starve. I sometimes ask them to dine with me. I really pity them, but pity will not fill empty bellies.

The Special Commission in Cork is hanging the people fast. Thirty-six have already swung, and now no man can be out of his house without a permit from the officer of the district, and this permit is just like one from Cork to Fermoy: 'Permit Paddy Lynch to proceed from Cork to Fermoy upon his lawful business and to be in force for three days and no longer — To all who may be concerned.' This is a part of the Insurrection Act. Will your neighbours believe this? But tell them it has not reached this province yet. I will send you the Act as a model for the Americans to adopt.

I walked out to Merlin Park.[7] Saw a great many rabbits but killed none. Mr. Stephens that drew Theophilus's picture in Dublin dined with me on Sunday. He seems a good sort of man and expresses great anxiety for Theophilus. He drew Matty's picture and it is very handsome. No frost or snow yet though this is March 4th, but we got rain enough. The water is now smooth over the long hedge in the river.

[March] 6th — I went out yesterday morning to the old race ground to hunt. I had only a few persons with me and Frank. I tried the new greyhound and she was be[a]t to pieces in the flat mountain near Lough Inch. Not a single turn, though she was not ten yards from the hare at starting. Frank made off to Ballymahon for he was hungry and Mr. and Mrs. [Bogonier?] was out but Master [B?] and the dear beautiful little babe were sitting by the fire, such objects as misery would call their own. A pig too, whom starvation might have taken as a model, graced the floor. Two hens and a burnt cat constituted the whole of the stock of this back woods man. Frank made out some waxy potatoes and salt herrings and Martin Mahon brought us ten penny worth of Poteen, and with the aid of Bog water we made a hearty repast and were not here till seven o'clock, being on foot more than nine hours. And this I did to cure me of a complaint in my bowels, and I thank God it had the effect, and I am well. Only think, Mr. Mahon had no turf. All he cut was wet. It was bogdeal we burnt to boil the pot. Tommy has 30 shillings gathered for to buy another mule for this unfortunate family, but where pig nor duck nor dog [n]or goose can live, what can we expect to do with this poor fellow and his family?

Mr. and Mrs. Burke and family are gone to St. Clerans. We lose a valuable and well disposed neighbour and friend. I hope Dudley has taken pains and wrote a letter of thanks to Mrs. B. If not, he has not lost any time, and I hope he now will for she eminently deserves it from him. I suppose your answer to this will tell me what you are fixed down to, as I assure you I long to hear that you are fixed upon the road to preferment.

I told you before that I paid £150 to keep Henry in his place in the Post Office and he still lives a burthen upon me. I offered William to get him into the East India Company's service, seeing that he was only fit for the Army and as the pay and allowance and *plunder* of the natives there is great. I thought he would be glad to be on the way to the title of Nabob, but he would rather be a lick plate to Sir Richard [St. George] and John Blakeney.[8] Robert has deserted me wholly, and with his little pittance and no industry has become another lick plate at Castleboy. But how shall I speak of another son, another lick plate. I knew that when he fell in with Judge Moore[9] and Colonel Hay and rode with the King I then saw and I believe told you that false pride had seized hold of him, and that he was lost. He squalled with his superior officer and because he was a Clerk (as it is called) he would not even for Judge Moore make an apology, and so he was obliged to resign out of the Post Office. True pride consists in doing what is right, and as he was in the wrong, true pride would dictate to him to make an apology. So here ends his campaign, and he now is living as a lick plate at Judge Moore's. So now I have at home I may say four lick plates for what else is Henry at his time of life, sponging upon me.

May I hope that my Dear Boys will reflect upon the melancholy fate of their four elder Brothers and take warning and keep wide of the rock they split upon, that they will look only to their own ability for their support in life, for having once obtained the capability to earn your own bread, you stand in defiance and independent of all men. But you will say that Robert is exempt from this charge, he has always lived with the Castleboy family, and he may, as Robert P. Persse is not married, be *yet* greatly provided for. To show you [the] folly of this, look at the past. Did they educate him? Did they give him a suit of clothes even in respect to his deceased aunt? And if they had no regard in his early day[s] for him, can they think of him seriously now? But to convince you of his folly, I need only tell you what poor William was once at Castleboy. He had a stable there, a horse and servant at his pleasure. It was said that Robert P. Persse made his will in favour of William and afterwards he wrote letters to him beginning thus, 'My dear heir at Law' and now all this friendship is forgotten and poor William seems as if the doors of Castleboy House were closed against him. [10]

I just now learn that Parsons has left Judge Moore's and gone to lick the plate of young O'Neill who has a lodge in the County Wicklow. See what a change from riding with the King and living with the Judge. Indeed I should be ashamed to see Lord Rosse after the conduct of Henry and Parsons. [11] When you write home, seem not to know these things, make no observation upon them. But let the fate of *your four* brothers work deep in your minds, for it is as a warning to you I make you this communication.

We have had a day dry, and I had a hunt and killed a hare at Merlin Park. Gilesey and Bondy ran well and will now be keen as I fleshed and bloodied them with the hare. It rains now again.

March 11 — No frost or snow this season. Three sods turf for one half penny and potatoes sixpence per stone, and no work. The poor famish. Pray let me know how they fare in your neighbourhood, what they eat for breakfast, dinner and supper, what appearance, what kind of house and clothing, as compared with this country.

Sad work. Warden Daly and Priest Daly [had] a great dispute about who should administer the last rights to old Hallyday. 'You lie' and 'you are a liar' came from the lips of Warden Daly, but he was provoked to that by the intrusion of the other. The Holy Oil and Water was knocked about, and Mr. Daly also quenched the Holy Candles and threw the Book from his hands. The Mayor and Sheriff were brought to the room to protect the Warden from the mob. Hallyday was buried, but a mob came in the night, dug him up, and took the coffin over the Churchyard wall and left it at Forster's door. Some people are taken up and very great sums are offered as a reward for the apprehension of the parties.

The Archbishop of Tuam[12] is in town and there is a complete split now between the two parties. God help us, our people [are] as ignorant as the Hottentots, and the advantages one religion has over the other, makes the two always ready for war, one to keep the ascendancy, the other to be ever placed upon a level with their fellow slaves or subjects. So you see what a gun powder mill we live in, for one spark would blow us all up.

Oh! Read the trials in Limerick and Cork and see what a state things are there. Read the evidence, I pray you, and the causes for which men are sent to Botany Bay, and let me know the American receipt for keeping people happy and quiet.

Poor nurse Peggy lost two Uncles drowned with a boatload of turf in the lake, boat and all gone. Their families are now beggars.

Theophilus, is *Badger* dead? Why do we not hear all about his exploits? The boys tease me to know all about *Badger*.

Richard, do they brew good beer in America? Can they brew in the severe frost and does the heat of summer stop them also? Is the barley and malt good? Do they use any brewing instruments I should say to ascertain the heat and gravity, or is it finger and thumb work with the Yankee brewers? I shall send you Shannon's guide for Young Brewers and I shall send you a copy of an old brewing book of mine, to keep that art in your recollection, even if it were only to be used hereafter for your own *private* use.[13]

Dudley, I hope you have selected your line of life, and, once done, I beseech you to lay your mind steadily to it, always recollecting that the rolling stone gathers no moss.

You will see by the public papers that England is disturbed as well as

Ireland and from the same cause, and that France is about to follow the revolutionary example of Spain and Portugal, that Italy and Germany are on the eve of revolt.[14] So that the battle of Waterloo nor the Holy Alliance could keep misruled Europe quiet, the example of untaxed, self-governed, happy America agitates the whole of the old states, and a man with any perception must see that until laws *such as America possesses* are universal in Europe, no peace or happiness can exist. Happy! Happy! boys to be removed from the bloody massacres of Limerick and the Martial Law system that transports one man to Botany Bay for having mud on his shoes, another because his heart beat quick when the policeman put his hand upon his side. And do not forget the fellow that was well dressed, and that had been in America, that was also transported because he was a *decent man.* Read these trials my Boys and see to what a state the Laws are brought to, and do get anyone to believe you that what the papers state *are true*, and thank God you are far removed from the effects of this terrible system. God keep it away from this town or else who knows where I may be sent to.

Take no notice of what I say about William, Henry, Robert, or Parsons in any letter you write home, as any remark of yours would not do any good. I stated the facts for to warn you from such conduct and to show you what an escape you had in this country, for had you stayed here in all probability you would all be lick plates in your turns.

Hoping, my Dearest Boys, that you will yet by your industry and propriety in life, raise yourselves up to independence in this life, and thereby give the close of my life some grateful recollections for all the anxiety I feel for you, and all that I have suffered in getting you out to the land of *the free* from this Island of Slaves.

> I remain, my Darling Boys,
> Your ever fond and affectionate Father,
> H. S. Persse

As I read on I like Mr. Darby's tour very much, but Mrs. Wright the Englishwoman's letters from America delight me. She is only to be surpassed as a female writer by Lady Morgan.[15]

[A postscript page, addressed to Theophilus, probably belongs with this letter. In Letter 4 HSP repeats its complaint against his sons' careless letter-writing style.]

To *Write is* not spelled *Wright*. There is no such word as *Wright* except the name of a hatter in Dublin, so spell *right* in future when you *write*, and recollect also that *no* one *knows* how to spell well who does not look at his dictionary. Now do you see how I brought in these words because you used them thus — 'Know *one here*' — when you ought to say *'No one here'*.

Now my Dear Boys, get Richard to look your copy over first. He will see faults that you cannot, and let you do the same when he writes. And if you disagree, your dictionary will set you right and decide. So now take more pains.

Letter 4

[Clement Sadleir arranged for Theophilus and Richard to enter a term of three years as labourer-apprentices on the farm of a Mr. Everett Yates in Johnstown, New York. Sadleir was a good friend of Everett's father, Horace Yates, both being involved in governmental and church affairs in Johnstown. The Yates family were prominent landowners in the county, Everett alone making twenty-nine real estate transactions between 1811 and his death in 1840.]

Galway March 15 18<22>

My Dear Theophilus,

Just as I made up the enclosed packet for the Boys and yourself I got yours and your Uncle's letter which gave us great joy to hear that Richard and you were settled for three years with Mr. Yates. But why Dick or Dudley would not write I know not, away so many months, passing over so large a part of the Globe, fixed down in a country where the detail of the most trifling circumstance would be to us most important, either as to manners, customs, dress, climate, food, fuel, kind of house, how made sports, wild fowl, deer, skating, sleighing, farming,

utensils — servants, their wages, how treated, barns what kind, threshing how done, wheat if good or bad quality, bread, cakes, fuels, pigs,
how fed, etc. etc. so that when you consider that the people here are
infants in knowledge about America, you cannot be too particular, and
I think if you were to say how an American Lady *regulates and manages
her house* and what she does, if her bedrooms are tidy or not (as Dean
Swift would enquire), in short I think there are ten thousand things that
you might write about.[16]

Never be afraid, my Dear Boys, as you practise you will improve in
spelling and style. I did not write so intelligible a letter at your age, so
do not be bashful. If you do not go into the water you will never swim,
and if you do not persevere in writing you will never succeed. Make
Dick read this several times over — for write you must all to me, and
if no other subject offers, give me the names of plants and trees and
their properties and appearances.

Your Mother is quite delighted at the thought of you being fixed. I
never saw pleasure so apparent in her countenance, for the conduct of
Parsons sinks deep in her heart, and your good natured Aunt Persse has
actually had her spirits quite depressed by the shameful conduct of your
brother Parsons. But what are these four? Are they any credit to themselves, or do they hold out any hope of rendering me any comfort in
my old age? Go on, excellent Boys, pursue in the satisfaction of the
Deity your honest endeavours and be not afraid but that I will have the
price of a house and farm for you when [you are] out of your time, if it
pleases God to spare my life. But I must expect before I do so or make
this sacrifice to hear from Mr. Yates most satisfactorily that you have
acquitted yourselves to his satisfaction and therefore are fit to take on
for yourselves.

I observe that Dudley has not yet fixed his mind, and this does not
at all displease me. I am far from wishing him to think that I would
impose upon him any pursuit in life that did not accord with his own
wishes. I think that although farming is the most healthful and certain
employment, and tends ever to rear up men to virtuous deeds, that still
it would be unjust in me to prevent Dudley making his own choice, but

at [the] same time it is my duty to advise. I think that the Druggist business is a right good one, better than that of a merchant, with less risk, but if the cotton or woollen manufacture is carried on in any respectable way I would like that he turned his mind to either, for I know and see that by the time he is of age manufacturing must be a *great* business in the United States, and there is no occupation in the world that I would prefer to manufactures when connected with agriculture or to say more clearly, a factory worked by machinery in a country place *with* a small farm adjoining.

What you say of eating three meals of meat per day and sweetmeats and preserves astonished my whole house. Never forget to tell us something upon this subject, for 'tis a hard blow against the oppressors of this country. But do not speak again in *general* terms. Give us a list of what you get to eat, for breakfast, and what to drink, and what for dinner, and enumerate also the kind of supper and drink for there are people here who think it is only wild beasts you eat.

The advertisement was funny enough. It afforded great surprise at first, but your Mother when she read your letter and your Uncle's ran off to the Widow Persse in joy to tell her all. Never was anybody so much changed for the better. I shall write your employer Mr. Yates and I am copying out or getting Sally to copy out instructions for you about Swedish turnip. It is what no Farmer should be without. Rape too will be of great advantage, but I know not how it will stand your frost and snow. It should be sowed a week later than the turnips and in drills of 18 inches or 2 feet and plowed between, so as to clean and mold up the plants. This might be cut down in the month of April and it would shoot up again and bear seed plentifully, but your climate I can't speak of with regard to rape, so that all kinds of trials should be made. If your ground is rich your ridges may be wide for then the plants will spread and cover the land, but if not, make the drills narrow. It is the best of plants for oil, and the cake or refuse from the mill after the oil is pressed out is capital food for horned cattle. Thousands of tons of this cake are shipped to England from many parts of Ireland for no other purpose but that of feeding cattle. Transplanted rape is best. It does well to do so after early potatoes, and if it stands your frost and snow *as it does ours* it would be then exactly fine green food in April and May for ewes and lambs and would be off in full time for a crop of barley to be sowed in. That is our way and thus have with ease three crops in two seasons and one more if you lay down with barley and *red clover*.

To *make* manure should be the *first* and *last* thought of a Farmer. Green crops and house feeding will effect that purpose. In summer I would keep cows during *severe heat* in the house all day, and out at night, and in winter in the house all night and out in the day when any food was to be had. A cow house should be a double house, the bales in the middle so that the cows in rows should stand with their heads opposite to each other, and a passage of 4½ feet wide should be left so as to enable a boy *(that is you)* to drive a barrow down the passage and feed the horned cattle at each side of you. If there are doors opposite this passage, dash goes the wheel barrow or asses car and the cattle are fed in a moment. Leaves should be gathered for litter but if bog mould is to be had when dry it answers very well. Burnt clay is one of the best and I believe with you will be found the *cheapest* of all manures where fuel is reasonable, and nothing gives so certain a crop of turnips and rape. You have a great advantage over us. The heat of the sun in summer and the severe frost in winter (if you do not spare the plough) must make any land good except sand. I like your ploughboy newspaper much. Read it regularly if you can — it will improve you. I hope Mr. Yates keeps a regular journal of the proceedings of his farm. It is absolutely necessary, and no Farmer will know what he is at if he does not see his produce upon paper as well as his mode of proceedings, expenses, etc. That I should like you kept. Ten minutes every evening, nay, half the time, would do all there could be to be said each day. This journal would, by entering upon it your experiments with rape seed, soon enable you to accommodate that plant to the best seasons for your climate.

Always prefer the drill husbandry to broadcast. In drills you can best mould up the plants, but stirring the earth between gives the roots room to extend farther in search of food, causes the earth to ferment and sends forth vapours that return upon the plants and refresh them with dews, kills all those weeds that if allowed to remain would rob your plants of so large a portion of your manure and thereby lessen your crop, so that the *drill is* the best if you will but plough between the rows occasionally for the purposes before stated, and it is also the cheapest mode of culture by far, as it saves both labour and seed. I hope Richard and you will learn to graft and bud fruit trees. My most excellent Father, who was an ornament to the first society in Ireland, could graft and bud as well as any gardener whatever, and my Uncle Taylor was also an excellent hand at this work.[17] And indeed I shall be greatly surprised if at the end of your three years you have not acquired a knowledge of surveying land, for according to my notions that man is unworthy to get a tract of land who, having had an opportunity to learn the mode of measuring it, knows not how much or how little he possesses. Would a man be fit to entrust with money that knew not how to reckon it? I will therefore send you one of the very best surveying instruments and a book of instructions and I shall expect you to make this science at school your study and, my Boys, when you arrive at manhood and are able to measure your own land you will be obliged to me for having urged you to acquire the knowledge of this art. And believe me it will prove more useful to you than if you were taught the fiddle. Mr. Mellish states in his travels in the United States[18] that a Mr. Zane, a surveyor of Wheeling, obtained as a remuneration for his services in laying out a state road in Ohio three most valuable tracts of land each a mile square. One is the plot upon which *Zanesville* stands, another that of the town of new *Lancaster* and some land at *Chillicothe*. Now my Boys, does not this show you that there is in America a reward for labour, and if after this advice and the example you have before you of your excellent employer, sure (when I desire it) [you] will not fail to acquire a knowledge of this art, for I would rather that you were perfect in this branch than that you got the Gold prize for Hebrew in Trinity College. For Hebrew, Greek, and Latin can do no good, but the surveyor who laid out the State roads or canals has done a lasting benefit to the human race, and more good than all the Trinity College chaps since the flood.

Besides, it would be such a disgrace to lads like you not to know all that your master (employer, I should say) is acquainted with. When I went to Cork I soon learned to spin cotton and then I got a loom and learned to weave. And without self praise, I did weave as smart and as well as any weaver we had, for I thought I could not call myself a manufacturer if I did not know how to spin and weave, and that feeling I thought sprung from *true pride*.

Judge Vandeleur is taken very ill and cannot go circuit, so now where are all the golden dreams of John Lambert? And I ask you now, is it not a dangerous experiment for any man to place his whole dependence in life upon the life or caprice of any man? See what a fall this is to John Lambert who made great preparations for the purpose and was at considerable expense to show himself out as a Judge's Register.

17 [March, St] Patrick's day. In all the old Governments there is a day laid out for folly. If it was a day devoted like the 4th July to the Goddess of Liberty, it would be a day celebrated by man as the day upon which truth and reason triumphed over tyranny and oppression.

In my life I never saw such a day of rain. I scarcely know how I shall get back to the house. It never ceased to rain the whole day so that Paddy will be wet inside and out, and I stayed at home the whole day!! The Tonabruckys are all gone, but I have three couple principally out of Spinner though [they] are not as good as the mother. However, I kill an odd hare. I killed one at Merlin Park, where Gilesey ran best, and I killed another above James Browne's when the Boys were in at the death. I took the hare alive. I saw she could not live so I tied up all the dogs but Bondy and Gilesey, gave her [*illegible*], and the Boys were delighted with the *little* hunt of their own, for the hare ran and by turning and twisting gave them great sport and Burty got the [*illegible*] which he wave[d] in triumph. And I had them out yesterday, and even had the good fortune to start a hare near Tonabrucky that ran plump into the middle of the Boys. Frank and Burty said that they could have killed her she was so near them, but they knew I would not be pleased.[19] The little dogs all had snaps at her and Spinner in the confusion was thrown. Even Ward's young pup was close to her. She however got clear off. We had a good hunt and *killed*, for it was a fine day, the *only fine* day I saw since you left me. Marcus was with me. He will go to you if you say what wages you can get for him. Write a few lines to Mark Carr of Tonabrucky and say what wages and *what kind of food you* can get for him, for he is very poor.

It is not to idle the Boys that I take them to hunt. It is to make them hardy men, fit for Yankee Land, for determined are the *three* boys to go to you. Burty says 'I made up my mind to go to America but not till I am a little bigger' and as to Tommy and Frank they would be off tomorrow if they could, and so would the two Lamberts. Mr. Burke has a grown up son at Athenry. He wants to go out with £500 or £800, but I say he would do no good. He knows nothing but about billiard tables, buttermilk love, and four corner chat, a mere idler at six feet high — too proud or too foolish I should say to put his hand to anything, so I desired his Father keep such a fellow at home.

My Dear Richard and Theo, I am greatly delighted that you are with so respectable a man as Mr. Yates and that you are *both together* is also a great satisfaction to me to learn. I trust, my Dear good Boys, that as you have ever lived in affectionate attachment that nothing will ever cause you to have the least difference with one and the other, but that you will by your brotherly tenderness for each other show that you are worthy to be associated together indeed. I do not suspect that you will ever cause me to regret your being together, but 'tis my duty to impress upon you this advice.

How thankful you should be to your really good Uncle. His anxiety, his tenderness for you, all is such that I never can forget. I could not avoid crying over his letter wherein he expresses his doubts whether you were lost or not, and the happiness he felt is most kindly told to me. He did not even forget the joy of poor Badger. The Widow P[ersse] was delighted with his letter. Now I just hear that there will be a vessel here from New York in May or June to Aty Lynch. She will go back in July. So now write directly to me a private letter to say what present you think would be most acceptable to your uncle that I could send out from this country to him, for I could wish to mark my sense of the obligation I owe to him for his never to be forgotten anxiety and kindness to you *three*.

I now get up early. I called Sally up at six, told her in a loud voice that Mrs. Yates was up an hour before, making cakes and preparing breakfast for Richard and Theophilus. The boys heard me and they laughed heartily. So you see my thoughts are as much at your side of the Atlantic as yours may be at this.

Let us have a state of your house. The Dutch were always remarkable for cleanliness, and let us have a regular *Bill of Fare* of a *breakfast*, a *dinner*, and a *supper*, who cleans shoes, who brushes coats, etc. etc. And do you ring the bell to have the candle snuffed as we do in Ireland? Will you believe that three men were hung in England the other day for shooting *partridges* and *hares*, and that the prisoners we have *now* in the hulks cost the nation more taxes to pay them than the amount of the whole expense of the civil government of America? No wonder that we are poor. You may imagine how little is known of your country when a man of Irish respectability asked me if there were *Judges* in the United States.

Watty Otter sends his love to his brother Dudley. He says he is quite anxious to see his new play fellow that is coming to him, Master Black Squirrel. Watty says he is tired of Dandy for he will not go with him to the dock to fish where he proceeds every evening, but after he fills his belly with his own catching is sure to return back every night to Mrs. Smith's where he sleeps. I have a hole in the door so that he can go in and out. My doves breed fast. Polly is quite well and she doats upon me. It still rains. John Lambert [is] in town, very low, poor fellow, for Judge Vandeleur is very bad. He wants me to see his father to consult about Robert and Charles going to you. They are darling boys and will have more than £1,000 each hereafter.

It is difficult for me to write to you. My collector is constantly away and Colonel Blake, poor man, is afflicted with a [burning?] gout that keeps him from the office so that I have the garrison to myself, or, in other words, all the bells are fixed upon one horse. Yet I continue to steal a moment from time to send you my thoughts, and I cannot avoid saying that all the sufferings I experienced in life are forgotten when I picture to myself the fond expectation of seeing my American Boys skilful, well informed, intelligent, persevering, industrious men.

What ever in this country has risen up, many great families, trace it back and you find that it sprung from the persevering industry of some one of their ancestry. Lord Erskine had been a midshipman at thirty-two when he left the Navy and studied the Law and reached the Woolsack or Lord Chancellor's seat, and no man ever yet who had determined perseverance that did not succeed in the object of his pursuit.[20] Be assured, my Dear Boys, it is the true road to the real comforts and enjoyments of life, and it is that certain independence that places you beyond the misfortunes that are attendant upon those whose support depends upon the disposition of others.

As I have to write to the Governor, to Mr. Yates and your Uncle, I must stop, hoping you got [the] King George the IV welcome buttons that I sent by the Dublin Packet, and that they will be in time for your Easter gift since they did not get in time for a Christmas box.[21] I leave the smaller folks to tell you the lesser news and I remain, my Dear Boys,

> your ever affectionate Father
> Henry S. Persse

Sally wants to know what time Mrs. Yates gets up, what hour breakfast, dinner, and supper, and what hour to bed.

I just find from Tom Coy that rape will stand any frost and snow whatever, and will be the best of green food for sheep in the scarce months of spring when the frost and snow goes away, and if fenced up after being cut down close it will shoot up again and bear a large crop of seed in August or September and the blosson will feed millions of bees before it gets into seed. He says the best time to sow it is from the < . . . > the 30th of June *in this climate* but I suppose later would do with you for fear that it might run to seed in your Indian Summer. I think it would be most valuable even as a vegetable for the table when no other can be had, as I learn that your frost destroys all others.

Letter 5

[*Reliable evidence of the extent of the 1822 famine in Connacht is scant. In this and the following letter HSP graphically attests to the extent of the distress, recounting his experiences in organising a food kitchen that served 1,500 Galway city families, and describing the 'hundreds of families' wandering emaciated through town. Recent estimates have suggested that death from starvation and fever in the region was limited in scope (see Introduction, p. 28). HSP, however, mentions here having personally seen a woman die 'of want at my window', and in Letter 6 refers to people 'dying like rotten sheep' in the streets or from eating 'sea weed or thistles' in desperation. His remarks give no indication of the actual number of starvation deaths, but suggest that it was certainly considerable. Letters written by the Archbishop of Tuam in June 1822 after touring Mayo and Galway (and published by Lady Gregory in Mr. Gregory's Letter-Box) report starvation deaths and nettle-eating, and urge immediate new help lest 'Thousands will die of actual hunger'. The archbishop's activism in obtaining relief monies resulted in grants of over £26,000 between June and August 1822, and his quick disbursement of these funds doubtless softened the hostility towards him voiced by HSP in this letter.*

As far as deaths from fever are concerned, HSP's commentary is considerably more specific here, listing the number of patients in the fever hospitals in Galway city, and referring in a matter-of-fact manner to numbers of friends and relatives who have been afflicted or died.]

Galway April 1 1822

My Dear Boys,

Yesterday I sent you via *Dublin* two letters dated in Febuary and March, and now I begin to write you my April dispatch. The Assizes are going on but I am not upon the Grand Jury, although Smyth was ordered by Mr. Daly to put me on the panel. This has incensed Mr. Daly, and Mr. Smyth has sent in his resignation, and we are to have new Sheriffs in September. William came to see us, so worn down an old looking rake you never saw, and his hand trembles like the aspen leaf. You, my Dear Boys, know well the cause of this, and I hope it will prove a lesson to you of more convincing a nature than anything I could write.

John Blakeney dined with us yesterday. I spoke much to him about rape. He says no frost will kill it and he prefers sowing it in drills to broadcast, *in very rich* land. The drills may be as far as three feet [apart], as it is intended for sheep feed upon the ground. Two feet would answer. I shall send some from Limerick and some from Dublin next vessel, and some of both kinds.

Two persons to be hung here *this morning* for murder, and thirty-five in Cork for execution. Can you match that in Yankee Land? The Judges were at church yesterday, dressed in their *robes* and *wigs* in order that the ignorant might wonder at them and imagine that they were more than human. They put me in mind of the Priests and Bishops dressed out at High Mass, and I do not see why mummery and nonsense should be retained or attached to our Courts of Law, no more than to our Church. But the fact is, that Interest makes Judges too, and to cover the blockhead it is necessary to give him some imposing dress so as to obtain for him that respect which his want of knowledge disentitles him to. And thus it is that these chaps are dressed out like Popish Priests to keep the ignorant in awe. I often wonder that these forms have not been improved upon since *Cook's* discoveries. A large painted feather run through the nose, the ear cut into stripes so as to hang upon the shoulder, beads in the hair, face painted, part tattooed, etc. etc. would give a *Judge* upon the bench a most *dignified* appearance.[22] I wish to know, is it the dress or the address or the sound sense and inflexible integrity that creates for Judges in America that respect which an administrator of Justice is entitled to? And I would like also to know, can you equal the Counties Cork and Limerick for murder, riot and confusion?

[April] 7th — The *Cuba* with flax seed from New York is arrived. She came quite unexpected to us as she sailed from you. However your mother, Matty and Sally got [*illegible*] by her and I got a book and some papers. The boys went off to get the Black Squirrel as a companion for Watty but were sadly mortified that they did not even get a letter from any one of you. And I fear that the *Cuba* will not go back to New York but proceed first from this to Oporto as the Master has been offered a cargo of wines there to take to New York.

I have written a long letter to Mr. Yates which I sent via Cork and I have confirmed your Uncle's agreement and returned him thanks for his kindness to you both.

I know not how you spend your idle moments. One would think that when I write so regular that you would reply. To think that here is almost May now and no letter from you since January's date. And to say you have no subject to write upon, when there is not a thing around you that an account of would not be acceptable. I wonder the welcome buttons of George IV did not make you speak, as you must have required some of them to make up your losses at sea. Theophilus, I hear, was so proud to hear cash rattling in his pocket, he went to bathe at [Fayal?], left his breeches on the beach and his money was stolen from him. Well done Theo. What did I buy a nice writing box for you for? And could you not have put up your money there? Dudley too must wear his watch in bed, no, but in his fob on board ship at the mast head, and down it came upon the deck, smash, when it ought to have been in his writing desk and then it would not be broke or left behind in the vessel.

John Burke is returned home. He gives a most shocking account of the country. The oats were chaff, the farms were woods, the sheep cats, trash of tea and coffee for breakfast, that he would have rather had potatoes and buttermilk, the people begging and coming in from all quarters to New York not able to get anything to do in the country, that John Hide the tailor was married and that he and his wife were begging in New York. He did not see a good ship but an English one, that Mr. Richard Sadleir[23] was in a very poor way — a petty apothecary shop like Cleran's in Loughrea. In short he stopped at nothing to make a story out to cover his own shame at returning home so soon, saying it was no country to go to, but, when he found potatoes 7½ pence per stone, he was thunderstruck to find the darling root so dear. He has made a fine campaign of it. No money now to pay for his passage and his watch, bed and wearing apparel all in pledge with the master of the vessel. He says he could have no luck in such a vagabond country, that it is no place at all for anyone to go to. Such lies never were yet heard, and all this comes at a time that distress and misery the most unbounded surrounds us.

We were bad enough when you left us now, but today potatoes are 8 pence per stone, and oatmeal 2 shillings per stone and turf four sods a penny, and fever rages all through the town. Mooney the tailor's daughter is dead of a three day's fever, so is Doctor McCue of the same complaint. The fever hospital is full and the Mayor committed 143 to the town jail where they are getting bread for doing nothing. The people in Connemara are obliged to fly. No potatoes there. The whole of the people of Innisheer Island have quit the island. Twentyfour are gone to America and many from the great island are begging in the streets. But what must the misery be in July next, before the new potatoes come in, if it is bad now?

April 15 — We have a fine change of weather. I never saw more beautiful weather after seven months rain. I sometimes take a hunt now and kill a hare too. I have a fine couple [of dogs]. My health was greatly affected by the confinement, but when I go out and take a long walk it improves. I meet no one able to stand it out with me. The Collector has been in the North of Ireland and is now gone to England and Colonel Blake is very seldom here so that I am quite a fag at the Customs House, and to mend matters there is ten per cent now taken off of my salary, that is £70. 8s. 0d. per year to be deducted from me in future.

John Browne our cousin is with me. He is the son of Captain John Browne of Carramore near Headford, whose mother was sister to my mother and my Uncle Blakeney of Abbert. Captain Browne married a sister of your Uncle Newenham and by her he had this son who will have a good property.[24] We had great sport with John Burke. He says a married man had no business to [go to] America, that he was too old to do any good, that Kentucky was 700 miles from him, and that it sure would take him ten years to get there.

Doctor Coffee and his family are in great distress. They have pledged all their things and are really at the last stage of want. What are we to expect from relations after this? What, the *Arch* Bishop of Tuam, a Cousin German with an income of £20,000 a Year and livings in his gift of thirty or forty thousand more lets his Cousin German starve in Galway after taking from him his curacy of £300 per year that that he enjoyed before *His Grace* got the Arch *Bishop Prick* of Tuam? Recollect this always as another proof of the indifference of relations towards their own relatives and also think of the inhumanity that makes poor Coffee now poor and in want because the stranger was removed and the relation filled his place.

[April] 20th — We continue to enjoy fine weather. The turf is getting dry and cheap but potatoes are eight pence per stone. Mr. [Bogonier?] has not one single morcel of food. We are obliged to support him. He has nothing but his fine boy and he offers him very often as payment to us for our kindness. I think the fellow is wild enough to be let loose among the Indians in America and I wish he were there.

[April] 23 — I send you a good many newspapers and also three little pamphlets that you may see how the religious war goes on. But I confess that my zeal for writing to you abates very fast when I recollect how negligent you are in writing to me, and I tell you plainly, if you practise your silence much longer, I shall treat you in the same way and drop writing altogether.

[April] 28th — Robert still at Castleboy. He never writes or says one word about you or any one of us. He cares not for tomorrow, so he has enough for the day, and I am convinced that the day is not far off when he will regret having so idly spent the summer of his life without a knowledge of how to earn his bread, or an income to support him in the line of life he ranks in, and like a kept mistress knows not the day he may be sent away to make room for some greater favourite.

[April] 28th — The Cuba has at last agreed to take passengers and go direct to New York. So now I do not pity you for not writing, for as you did not write I know not what you want, so can send you nothing. Blame yourselves. I just heard that one of the Liverpool Packets was lost — The Albion, near Kingsale. So if you wrote by her your letters are lost. This shows you that you should write one letter to be lost and another to come safe, as I do. I am endeavouring to get a good ram and ewe to send out in the Cuba, and I shall send some more rape seed by her.

[April] 30 — Mathias that kept the little shop near the bridge, he that served his term to Arthur Marshall, is going to New York. He is an honest creature and if he falls in your way, recommend him. Morris's miller whom I understand is a very clever fellow goes also and takes *Mathias* with him.

I believe if Mr. Lambert was at home (but he is in Dublin), that he would send out Robert Lambert by this vessel, for Robert is very anxious to go. Wat would be very glad that he was sent for they have no hope at home and distress is fast increasing, and many wealthy families are gone to France to live. Mr. French of Monivea says in his letter to Doctor Veitch that he wonders how any one that has any means to quit would live in the vagabond climate of Ireland among our overtaxed, famishing, cut-throat people, when for a trifle they can enjoy all the luxuries of life in France. Mr. O'Hara of Raheen lives in Naples and will never come back. Mr. Gregory of Coole, Lord Ashtown, Mr. Daly [*illegible*], Eliza Blakeney, Lord Clanmorris, and hundreds more of the wealthy who have run away from the taxes, and while this is going on among the rich, here are three vessels taking out working people to America.[25] One ship put in here from Dublin has upwards of 360 passengers on board bound for Quebec.[26] So you see that rich and poor are running away from the rents and the tythes and the taxes, and God help them that must stay at home and pay *their* share and their own share till they come back.

May 2 — The 4th of July will be near at hand by the time you get this letter. I know it will be kept with proper respect at Johnstown and as you are to be American Citizens, I hope you will pay proper respect and devotion to that day, and that you will write me a full account of everything that occurs upon that day and how you like the manner in which a Nation of Freemen celebrate the day of their independence.

I hope you will let me know if you are to learn land surveying. It would be a proud moment of my life the day I heard that you were competent to survey a large estate. The word in America is 'What can you do?' 'Sir, I can farm land, plow, sow, thresh, mow, and cut down a tree or drive a waggon, graft and bud fruit trees and can survey land.' Here would be a recommendation. Better far than what young men rely upon here, namely a head and stomach to bear twelve tumblers of punch or four bottles of wine. I therefore feel happy and proud that you three will be brought up to virtue and industry and that I shall be yet proud to think I am your Father. In China, honours are the *reverse* of what they are here. *Here* the glorious actions of a man *descend* to his Children but there the meritorious conduct of the Child is rewarded in the person of the Father, for his having brought up his Child so well, and as a future inducement to others to imitate his examples. And when both die, the title ceases.

May 4 — I need not tell you what ruffians are called to the Peerage here, nor the causes for which they are ennobled, as it is called. That is not my object, but if you recollect that I shall feel in my own heart myself ennobled by your virtuous conduct, and as I know you love me, I hope and trust you will make me *inwardly* a Duke, by hearing that you act in a way to gain me credit.

May 5 — The poor or rather the operative classes here are in the greatest possible distress. It is impossible to give you a just picture of such misery as now walks abroad. The moving spectres are like walking deaths, a woman just now expired from want at my window. Potatoes are 9 pence per stone this day. The system of starvation in the midst of plenty cannot, must not, last long.

Think my Dear Boys of the system that raises so much money in taxes from the Farmer as to leave him no possibility of being able to pay his rent and then lends him back upon pawn of his corn a part of these same taxes for his relief, with an intent to raise the price of his corn, and then raises more taxes upon the Farmer to distribute to societies for the purpose of selling out corn at a reduced price to *lower* the price of that same corn for the relief of the poor, and the ruin of the Farmer. So here you see a fine system of mish mash, taxing all parties to ruin, and then applying new taxes to raise the price of corn for the benefit of the Farmer, and lowering it for the benefit of the poor. In the same manner we borrow to add to the national debt, and we tax the nation to pay off the same amount in the same year, and employ two boards of Commissioners, one to increase the debt five millions and another set to pay off the like amount, and pay large sums annually to the people who collect the taxes to pay off the five millions and premiums, bonuses, discounts and interest to the jews and jobbers that lend the like sum to increase it. Do you now wonder that we are a nation of beggars and oppressors, that we are continually in a state of insurrection and that we require a large army to keep the people in awe. But I will trust my pen too far upon this subject.

There is to be ten per cent off of salaries. I lose by this £70. 8s. 0d. per year, but I think nothing of this as I am in hopes that the retired salaries for superannuated officers will be more permanent and I do not hope to be always in the Customs House. I send you one guinea in gold for each of you and I hope you got the nine gold sovereigns I sent you before. And indeed I must and cannot avoid saying that you do not deserve these three guineas that I now send when you deny to write to me a single line since January last, and here is the twelfth of May now that I am writing upon, and no one in the Customs House but me to do all the business. Yet still I do not plead want of time to write to you. I send you the very last Mrs. Connolly in this package that you may see what she says about the distress that we are in. If you have any thought you will now bless your stars that you are away from want, misery, plague, pestilence and famine, and that industry where you are receives its just reward.

Adieu, my Dearest Boys. May heaven continue its blessings toward you, and that you with grateful hearts may ever acknowledge the manifold goodness you receive at his hands and may faithfully, virtuously, and industriously so employ your time as to show your gratitude for the whole period of your lives is the constant prayer of

> your ever fond and affectionate Father,
> Henry S. Persse

I beg to be remembered to Mr. Yates and his family to whom I wrote via Cork last month. I send another bag of rape seed, of the common kind, same as Theophilus took out. The ram and ewe I now send are most beautiful creatures, but two years old. Bill Smith goes to take care of them in the Cuba.

Letter 6

[This letter, HSP's longest and most remarkable document, provides powerful evidence of the severity of the Galway famine of 1822. It details the part he personally played in relief efforts, specifies the numbers of people receiving relief in Galway city or currently in the fever hospitals, and offers a sustained critique of the socio-economic structures that allowed starvation to occur 'in the midst of plenty'. The experience of taking in a starving three-year-old child, Polly Geary, who with her siblings had been left 'like a deserted cat to perish in the streets', affected him particularly strongly, and in this letter he holds her up as a prime example of the way true potential was being crushed by an unjust system in his country. Ill-nourished, speaking only Irish, and separated from her mother and brothers, she nonetheless showed an innate genius and charm which for HSP obviously confirmed his views about the evils of primogeniture, 'Interest' and class divisions, and which only served to strengthen his belief in the advantages his sons might enjoy in America.]

Galway Ireland
July 10 1822

My Darling Boys,

There has been a great chasm in our correspondence owing to your not writing as regular as I could wish, but any anxiety is now relieved by the receipt of your letters of the beginning of April that we received yesterday, and I have to hope that you will never neglect us again for so long a period as you have done, but that you will write regularly in future.

The distress of this country is beyond description. You knew what it was before, but judge what it must be when there is not a single vile potato to be had around us, and when the oatmeal is entirely exhausted. I have my own trouble, up everyday at four or five o'clock, my stick I cast away, and wear a short jean jacket and trousers with drawers, busy as possible having in addition to the *whole* charge of the Customs House, 1500 families to feed with bread and soup. I buy wheat at the market, get it ground, pay a baker for making it into bread, buy small bullocks at the fairs, and with some oaten meal, pepper, and onions, I make excellent soup. The parties applying have tickets, signed by the priest. I have a large yard and as they come in I give them their portion and when all are served I open the doors and all go away. A quart of soup and half a pound of bread is the allowance. This barely keeps them alive. There is bread and buttermilk stored in the Lombard Barracks[27] where 3,000 strangers are fed, but all mine are townspeople. I have Mrs. Smith, [Nina?], Peggy, and Betty at the soup shop, and Frank's nurse has the contract for buttermilk. There are stores open for the sale of cheap meal to persons having tickets of poverty are allowed to buy, and at these stores whole ground wheat meal is sold at one shilling per stone, barley meal the same, but oaten meal at 18 pence per stone.

This gives but little relief, for the crowd that assembles round the stores keeps poor creatures there the whole day for threepence worth of meal. Some have their legs and ribs broken. Such a scene is not to be looked at in any other spot on the globe except at the soup shop when the door which I call the flood gate of misery is opened, and although I have now regulated it so that it is the *last in* that *is first* helped, yet such is the anxiety that the moment the door is opened, if I had not three or four great strong men at the door to keep the pressure back, I should have scores of men, women, and children trodden to death.

When this is over I go to the Committee at the Tholsel that meets every day at three o'clock and breaks up at five or six. Here we have long debates, in which I take no part, as long speeches to hungry bellies is but bad food. I take a great share though in the correspondence, and in the Select Committee for employing the poor I have been of use. I prevailed upon them to undertake the road to Bally Mahon, also from Barna to Lough Inch, and to Tonabrucky and from Castlegar though the bog adjoining Claregalway river to Annaghdown, and all these roads will be made fit for the mail coach to travel upon. So I hope that we shall have turf cheap in future.

But to what good is this momentary benevolence of the English people, when you consider that the wages are cut down to 8 pence per day or 4 shillings per week and as we have three days out of the six wet so that the working creature gets but two shillings per week on an average after having, as he says, himself eat[en] his clothes, pig, fowls and fur-niture. All this benevolence is to cease on the 16th of August. How will it be then for he that could not sow his potato garden this year for want of seed potatoes [having] after planting dug up the seed to allay hunger? So many come in and speak to me that you see I cannot write correctly, for in the absence of Colonel Blake and [Mr. Collier?], all the weight is upon my back.

There has been an addition built to the fever hospital and tents pitched in the yard to hold the numerous diseased, but that's not enough, for the Lombard Barracks is also to be an hospital for the fever patients. See what famine in the midst of plenty does. The people are dying like rotten sheep. Oh that some of your neighbours could see the hundreds of families that wander about, pale, emaciated, those whom hunger has rendered appalling, and whom famine has devoured to the very bones and ligaments. To see these creatures in a waste house bun-dled together like pigs to keep each other warm, for if they had means, no one would let them in for fear of infection! I took in 5 miserable children whose father and mother were sent to the Fever Hospital. They were left in the street like birds in the snow to perish. I fitted up the turf house for them, and such spectres I never beheld. When they got food, dysentery followed copiously with blood, and the eldest, so like Theo, paid the greatest attention to the little things, took fever also, and we sent him to the hospital *out of* our house.

The youngest was upon the mother's breast when the poor woman was sent to the hospital, but the second youngest, Miss Mary Geary, is without a doubt the most surprising child at three years old (*though only speaking Irish*) that I ever saw or heard of. She sings true and sweetly. Every word she expresses has some action with it, to better explain her meaning. She is a little player in miniature. She was asked which she liked, Matty or Sally, best. She said that Sally was handsome, but, throwing her arms back and extended, she explained that she liked Matty best, though Cook said she must be a Fairy — in Irish, 'Her soul but she was' was the reply — that she spent a year at Castle Hackett, she was with Finnavarra (who is, they say, King of the Fairies), that she rode upon a white horse that had but one leg, and that that leg was a wooden one, that she was at the races of Knockma where every Fairy had a race horse, and thus with her stories (Mr. Morris her interpreter) she has won the whole house and your mother has her constantly in her lap and is delighted with her.[28] She visits boldly all the neighbours, sits at Mr. Daly's in his lap laughing out of the window, turns up her nose at the beggars and says what dirty creatures they are.

Just now pause and reflect. Here was a little female child, that if educated and taken care of had all the essentials to be a Queen, left like a deserted cat to perish in the streets, and this is the system that is 'the envy of surrounding nations and the admiration of the World'.

But English generosity has interposed and sent relief, and what relief is it? Some of the same food that in our poverty, early this season, we were obliged to send away though we knew we should want in the Spring. But what does all this generosity amount to? A few thousand pounds sent here to relieve the starving people. Why send any? Why not leave the people their own? Give me the duties or taxes paid by Pat Joyce or John Kelly and Stephens, and I would make more improvements and give more relief than all that will be done here with English generosity and the munificence of a *Paternal* government.

Mrs. Burke has taken example by me, and has eighteen of the starved and deserted children to take care of. But I could get her 1800 if she could protect them. They are lying about under the beams, back of the wall, and by the sides of ditches without covering, and will it be believed that *generally* speaking human sustenance never was so plenty or so cheap at any period for the last thirty years as it is at this moment? But it is money that is reduced in quantity, that paralyzes all our endeavours, for with a contracted currency and the same portion of taxes to pay, all men are on the brink of beggary. The man who paid his tax of £30 per year with ten sheep a few years ago now gives thirty sheep to pay the same sum or tax, because the price of fat sheep now is 20 shillings each, instead of £3 per [sheep], what it was lately. So it is with wheat, oats, turf, barley, bullocks, horses, etc. and if you turn this in your minds and converse upon it, it will enable you to explain the causes of the distresses of *this* country. Whenever the subject is spoken of, it will solve the riddle or paradox of people starving in the midst of abundance.[29]

Money, or circulating medium as it is called, is like blood in the human body. If you stop or even contract the circulation, debility follows. Money is not food, yet all starve without it, as barter could not answer the purposes of exchange. T'would be hard to buy shop goods with wheat, turf, sheep, corn, and potatoes. Blood to appearances as a fluid contains no strength in it, yet bleed the strongest man plentifully, or stop the circulation of that blood, and no infant so weak as he is immediately. Now, my Darling Boys, if you did not know these things you would appear ignorant among strangers, you could not appreciate the blessings around you. For be assured that with all your boasted comforts and happiness in America, let your circulating medium be fixed at its present amount, and let Irish tythes, rents, and taxes to be levied upon you, and I swear that Irish Misery will be the result at once.

I anticipate great pleasure in the perusal of Dudley's Journal. I feel so anxious to know everything about your adopted country, for here there is so much ignorance about everything of America, 'All a wilderness inhabited by people who live by hunting and dressed in skins, the few Farmers that are in it are no better than Irish freeholders of Connemara.' So that every thing that contradicts such nonsense opens the eyes of prejudice and has its effect.

I hope Mr. Moore's example will have a good effect upon Dudley. Mrs. Lambert of Castle Lambert made shoes for her whole family, and Lady Clanmorris, you know, makes beautiful boots and shoes. Your Uncle Newenham is never so happy as when he has his chest of tools and is at work as a carpenter, and you saw on the young Lamberts coats made of the cloth their mother manufactured. In good old times, *your* fashion was *ours*, but now we cannot even brew our own beer, tan leather, make malt, grow hops, shoot or hunt without a tax first paid, and this is what makes us so poor and what caused me to send you across the great waters where the fruit of your own labours could be gathered for your own benefit, and not applied to feed and support the idle, the profligate, and the insolvent. Read about the Bishop and the Soldier in the public house in London and ask your neighbours how would they relish that the tenth of their property and their industry should be given to a Sodomite.[30]

Theophilus speaks often of Fonda and Langsine in his letters.[31] In his next let him explain, tell us who these are, give us a view of the household, family, and farm, names, ages, style of house and furniture, clean or dirty, acres, crops, stock, number of hands employed to work it, what kind of offices, whether tidy or otherwise, garden, orchard, etc. so that we may see into your whole system and learn who are your compeers. The mode in which your female associates fill up their time I should like much to learn. A good and full account would read an excellent moral lesson to your female acquaintances at this side [of] the globe.

Let Mrs. Yates and Mrs. Moore know that a few years ago Mrs. Lambert preserved fruit with honey instead of sugar, and that I eat the other day some of the sweetmeats, as good as ever I tasted at Castle Lambert. They were not dried fruits, but wet, in jars.

Watty B[lakeney] is in irons aboard the Pl[?] for some very bad business!!

I am glad you have seen no soldiers. Man is prone to peace. 'Tis only when measures contrary to reason and justice are sought to be enforced that military aid is required. All men will readily associate for the protection of Society and the security of each other's lives and properties, and what more is necessary? But, agree to pay 8 Guineas an acre for burnbeating, consent to tythes and 6 shillings per gallon upon whiskey, 4 shillings and 4 pence per pound upon tobacco, 15 shillings and tuppence per barrell for every 12 stone weight of malt, and then you will require soldiers to collect the rent, the tythes and the taxes, and in the conflict to get from those unable to pay, a bloody civil war would ensue, and soldiers, Peelers,[32] Revenue police, and waterguards must be employed. And when numbers in any state are employed and paid for in unproductive occupations by those who labour, beggary, misery, and want must follow so long as the drones are allowed to suck the honey which the working bees had collected. Study this and you will see the whole cause of our sufferings.

As Mr. Yates thinks my ideas about the root of misery strange, coming as they do from the only Irishman who has ever exclaimed against potatoes, I think I am called upon to reply and explain my reasons for wishing to see this root abolished from the *general* use of Irishmen. Potatoes require great manure and tillage. The best lands and the greatest portion of dung is used in their cultivation. Lands that would give wheat or oats without any manure are appropriated to their culture. The crop when raised acre for acre does not contain (although *bulk* says the contrary) as much nutricious aliment as wheat or oats, and if an unpropitious season follows one that had been superabundant, the whole people starve, for who ever heard of potatoes of even the former year being available to meet or supply the defect in a present one? Can potatoes like wheat, oats, barley, rice, or Indian corn be held over for even fifteen months to make up the deficiency in a short crop? If they could, where could stores be got to lay by the unwieldy article? Not so with corn and grain. They can be preserved for *many years* and lie in a small compass too. So the famine of one year may be guarded [against] by a hoard in the previous one. Again, wages are regulated by the prices of the principal food which the operative classes subsist upon. And thus it is that Ireland, unfortunate Ireland, is paid by the Potato Standard of from 4 pence to 10 pence per day, never mind the effects. A wet season, a dry summer, or a severe and early frost destroys the whole crop. What is then to be done? The Irishman sees that he had been fed upon the lowest scale of human sustenance, and paid at the poorest wages. Potatoes gone!! which his wages could only [just] reach!! What is he now to do? Is there any cheaper food? No! except sea weed or thistles. If he eats these (as has been the case here), death follows. Can he who has been fed and paid by the scale of the root of misery all of a sudden *ascend* to bread, beef and beer? No, he cannot. And although these may be as they are now in superabundance, he may starve in the midst of plenty, as is the case this moment all around me, whereas if bread and beef and porter were the standard of wages and the food of Irishmen and scarcity of these [were] to take place, he would have room to descend to a cheap substitute for a while and he having better wages could afford to meet the calamity. Besides, foreign nations might relieve him. He would be able to send to America or France for a supply of flour, or to India for rice. But I wish to know would potatoes bear the expense of freight, and what country could send him a supply, or would all the shipping in Europe hold sufficient for seven millions of people to subsist upon for six months? Again, what must Mr. Yates think of a people without any artificial wants? The Irishman and the Pig are here upon the same level — the same food, the same bed (straw), and the same hovel — neither knowing anything about artificial wants or desires. If the potato eating creature could afford to consume any luxury whatsoever, had any kind of furniture in his house, in a year of scarcity he could cease to use them and apply his whole means to feed his family. But do, my boys, now take up the subject for me, and lead Mr. Yates up to Ballymahon, and give him a peep into the artificial consumption of Mr. [Bogonier's?] house and family, and tell him of the boy that exultingly said, 'from his Soul, it was not a year ago since he ate bread before'.

I dare say you know how warmly attached my Father was to the American Cause and how sincere his friendship for General Washington whose picture hangs up in my drawingroom. I now enclose you a copy of one of the General's letters to my father. It is the only one out of many that he wrote that I could as yet obtain, and I request that you will have this letter published in the New Jersey or Johnstown paper, as I do not find that in the life of Washington my Father's name is mentioned. I hope to obtain the rest and to send you the copies, for the originals are too valuable to send across the Atlantic. I request you will send me a newspaper having this letter in it.[33] I do not expect nor hope, nay nor do I wish your advancement in life by any other means than your own merit. Still it must be to your credit and advantage that your Grandfather was such a friend to the General, and that he lent his aid to establish and promote that independence which you, my boys, are now reaping the benefit of, and which I pray God you may know how to appreciate when you contrast it with the misery and vice of this distracted country. You see, my Dear Boys, that my Father thought well of America. Therefore it is not surprising that I should have turned my eyes there to seek your independence.

There are great changes in the Revenue. The Commissioners are to be dissolved and the Board held in London. The window tax is repealed and all that gang, of which [Pease?] is one, are to be sent to the right about.[34] Such long faces as are to be seen among those to be turned out, and those that expected to get in, that hope even itself has fled from them. The Excise and Customs will be united in all small places, so that both will be held at the Customs House and Mr. Reilly be the Collector of the one and other. So you see what a stew all the Revenue and expectancy people are in. They thought to live a life of idleness, upon the industry of others, but now all their hopes are blasted. Too lazy to work, and too proud to beg, they are famishing in silence. More taxes will be taken off, for the people cannot pay them, and hundreds more of the tax-eating crew will be sent adrift. Robert wants to get to be a Barony Constable under the new act, but it is only half pay people that will be appointed.[35] This boy is full of the pride of idleness, but I dare say that you would not wish to exchange now with a police constable in Ireland, a man employed to hunt down the peasantry and see that they are in their houses after sunset, and not out before sunrise, agreeable to the Insurrection Act, and force them to pay rent, tythes, and taxes. A fine trade for what is called a Gentleman.

We see everyone here going down the hill. Will you state (Mr. D. S. Persse) how Mr. Moore began, what he had beginning, and what he is worth now, and give us a little insight into his family, farm, mode of living, stock upon his land, etc. etc. and how many hands work it.

July 25 — I just received your letters of May and beginning of June and I know not how to express the gratification we all felt at the pretty manner you have expressed yourselves, and the joy we feel at your being so happy. Theophilus's letter made a most sensible impression upon your Mother. Indeed, I never knew her so well as she has been since she received it. But in saying this I do not mean to detract from

Richard's or Dudley's merit, as all the letters are equally gratifying and I know not to whom the palm is due. I like the notion about the sheep very much, and I will never let any opportunity slip of sending the best kinds to you, such a breed as those by the Cuba, which I hope are safe with you 'ere this, as well as a few more of the welcome buttons I sent by her. I am fully convinced from what you say of American and English mutton and the great disparity in the prices, that a Farmer that would breed sheep for the purpose of hiring out the rams (or tups as they are called) would make a good income of the business. It was by that trade that Mr. Wade made all his money.[36] Twenty to eighty guineas for the season is or was the common hire of a ram to tup ewes, and still [is] in this country. He makes a great deal of money. I will send one or two of his breed. They are different from those I sent before, and when you are out of your times I will get a shepherd from Wade's to send to you to instruct you in the care of rams and in all the schemes, or jockey-like work that is practised to set them off to the eye, and in the shearing and clipping, hiding every defect in the shape by not exposing the hollows in the carcass or back, but shearing in so nice a way as to make the back straight, the body round, the neck fine, the offal [*illegible*], all which requires as much jockeyism as ever was practised by a Yorkshire farrier in the sale of a horse. The feeding, the care etc. etc. etc. is all I assure you a science with the gentlemen of the turf society, and money they make by their trade every year regularly, much more, and with much less trouble than the *high bloods*, that say 'pon Honour I would not disgrace myself by hiring rams, if I were to make thousands by it — the word "Ram" is so indelicate it makes me blush, I declare'.

But such notions you do not possess, and I seriously think that I shall be able to send you over a good many every year, and that the breeding of the best kinds will be a very good business. I should like to know are the sheep in America subject to staggers, red water, scale, lameness, rot, or what other complaint, for in this country they die in hundreds of these disorders.

Mr. Wade's plan is to have his lambs *early*. They are of course *older* than his neighbours' lambs, and people, not knowing this, wonder that his are so much *larger* than their own. Then, when he shears, he does not cut as close as others, but shears early, and his lambs by this have an inch perhaps in appearance beyond those otherwise managed. And so in minding everything, in care, breed, management, and skill, he beats the whole county, and makes money by his superior attention to his business and his sheep.

I will send out the flower seeds and garden seeds to you by a vessel in January from Liverpool, so that you may have them in time. And I now give you due notice that there will be a vessel here from New York early next spring that will take anything you may have to send. She is to be loaded to Messrs Burke by Barclay's House in New York. The catching of the pigeons amused us much. We wondered at the smoke house. Pray let us know what kind these pigeons are, woodguests or house pigeons, colour and size.

[July] 28 — I hope I shall hear a full account of the agricultural meeting and show that is to be held at October in your county. That is what I admire beyond horse racing, boxing, or any other of our idle and vicious sports. I hope you will be there and that you will contrast the appearance of the people there with those you left behind you. Let me know how goes on the canal, and when it will be finished.

[July] 30th — I have every day told at the house that I was about to write and send off my letters but I can get no one to begin their letter to you so that I fear all the small news will be forgotten.

Aug[ust] 2 — In May and June we had very hot weather, but the latter end of June and beginning of July were very wet. I thought we should see another deluge but the weather has cleared for the last fortnight and I *guess* we shall have great crops. Neaty Clancy is dead. Mrs. Berry, Mr. Tighe of Newfield and his steward, and many more of the fever. Doctor Coffee is travelling all over the wilds of Connemara, employed attending the sick poor in fever, for which he is paid by Government. He wanted it much, I assure you, for he is still an unemployed curate.

August 4 — This day twelve months [ago] my Dear Boys sailed. I do not forget the day and after that my anxieties commenced. If I suffered enough in my anxiety about you during your voyage, I am now repaid by the sensible determinations my boys have put on, and the comfort I feel in having them removed from famine and fever and from a country where all trades are beggars. John Browne, son to my cousin, John Browne of Carramore, has been at my house these four months. He is a most excellent young man. He is very companionable, and he and your Mother have many joking wars and squabbles. He has drawn three likenesses of mine, which go to you by this conveyance as his gift. I dare say he will send others. Morris is not yet returned from America. We expect packages by him from you.

[August] 5th — I endeavour to keep the newspapers for you but it is very hard to do so, Mrs. Connolly is in such demand. I send a good many by this conveyance. It will soon be time for me to send another lot of boys out. Tommy I think it would be wise to fix in New York to business, and he might be serviceable to you living there. Frank says he must be a Farmer and Burton is too young to ask him yet his opinion, but I should like to know what you think as to the best age for to put boys to business in America and when I ought to send them out. For if I was inclined before to do so, surely events now must determine me in the resolution, for all classes here are in a bankrupt state which, added to partial famine and pestilence, must induce every man of mind to wish to quit the country altogether. And thousands are quitting everyday, the rich to France and the poor to America. I refer you to the newspapers about the fever hospital and the Lombard Barracks, now a house of recovery.

August 5th — Sporting intelligence. I still keep a few dogs and hunt once in every eight weeks. Spinner has three pups. Bondy and Gilesy ready to have more. I got ten brace of hares this year all of which I let out in the Recorder's desmesne. He intends to complete the wall and to add twenty acres more to his quantity of land. If he preserves them I will soon find plenty of them to fill his parks. John Browne kills an odd salmon with three hooks. He could not kill one any other way. Keogh takes no notice of him doing so. William does nothing. He gives himself too much to the bottle ever to reform and now I see no hope whatever of his getting any situation. Henry is worse. He went to Loughrea, gave some man there the lie at a hazard table and for which he received a fine painted face so bad that he could not show for ten days. I certainly will turn him out of the house. I will not put myself to expense to support him in vice and drunkenness. He has cost me enough already, money that ought to be now laying by to purchase you a farm. I know not what Parsons is about. I advanced money long ago to bind him to an Attorney, but I declare this moment I know not what he is about or whether he is bound or not, so silent is he. Robert never comes near us but once from Castleboy with me for the last twelve months. So you see how these four lads are. From any *one* of whom have I the least hope of their doing good? So sure as it is day R[obert] P[arsons] Persse will never do more for him than teach him to live a luxuriant idler. And what will be his lot when he leaves Castleboy? He would have now no more business to [go to] America than a Turkey Cock would have to go to swim to [the] Arran Islands.

August 6 — Bobby Molly, the bastard, thank God, is out of the agency of Roxborough. Mr. Wade of Fairfield, that is brother-in-law to your Uncle Robert, is agent. No account can be rendered or got from Smyth or Bob of the agency accounts during their time or since I gave up that charge.

August 7 — And now, my Dear Boys, I have my most pleasing task to perform, that of informing you what happiness it gives me that you take cheerfully to your labours, that you seek practically to be good Farmers, and that you have banished from your minds all those foolish and unprofitable notions which are the fashion of this country. I believe you know that it could be no pleasure to me to cause you trouble, that I would work my bones to the stumps to give you a life of ease and competence, but as you say yourselves, where is affluence to be found without great industry. In the Navy? What a life! For months at sea upon salt provisions, and if promotion offered, none but Interest obtains reward. And see how few stick to it for any length of time. And is the Army better? Merchants here as well as Farmers are all broke. Those who spent an age at the calling are as poor today as when they started. Places under Government? You see a good example in your brother William, who has been upon the list of promise for the last nine years and now has not either the money or ability to buy or earn a pair of shoes for himself. So that, my Dear Boys, the more you think of this country, the more ought you to be satisfied with your present situation. There is besides room in the States for men to prosper without injury to their neighbours, no one to envy your prosperity, or to [*illegible*] upon your industry by a disposition to tax it with more rent or tythe in proportion as that industry enabled you to pay better.

I long to know have you a pound for cattle to be confined in America, or are you so cruel as to starve the animal for obeying the call of hunger, or submitting to the will of its owner. Let me be fully informed of this.

August 10 — Your Uncle Burton is alive and well, keeps his hounds as usual, and lives near Roxborough where Regan the priest did. He was asked why he came back to that neighbourhood. 'Why,' says he, 'I am like the hare. It was here that I was first started. I took my ring, the world hunted me, and I am making home to die near my old form [lair of the hare].' Not bad from an old sportsman.[37] Robert Newenham has quitted the Army in India where he had double pay. No one in this country will receive him. His Father was in jail in France, his Mother in Dublin in great distress and very ill.

August 11 — My pets are besides dogs, two young deer, one young otter, two Cornish daws from Arran, two wood thrushes from Castle Lambert, six doves, one fine house owl very tame, one stair or starling, Polly, the linnet, and Miss Mary Geary. Spinner has three pups. Bondy and Gilesy ready to tumble. I keep no greyhound and will send all the dogs away but those of Spinner's size.

August 12 — The only Coy alive, James Coy, lives at or near Louisville, Kentucky. I believe he will never do any good for he is given to drink, of which his Brother died. I just heard that the Cuba got safe to New York but did not hear any thing else. Coy sometimes stops at Shelbyville in Kentucky, so just try that place upon your letter. I sent you some most valuable rape seed by a vessel from Limerick. I hope you got it safe and that you sowed it. You ought to get a great deal of money for that seed, for it sells here at 5 shillings per ounce. I sent you some of the common kind by the Cuba as well as Cobbett's *Gardener*. I have the *Farmer's Journal* and Tull's *Husbandry* to send you, and any I think that will be of use I will send.[38] Tull is a first rate book. Mr. Cobbett praises it highly. William has a fine ram lamb rearing for you at Abbert. He is certainly very good natured, but he drinks too freely and has a bad head. This harvest promises to be most abundant notwithstanding all the rains we have had. It has recovered by the fine weather we now have and will be very abundant and good.

I feel forever obliged by your Uncle's affectionate kindness to you all. It has made an indelible impression upon my recollection, and, my Dear Boys, I long most earnestly to know what I should send him per next vessel, as an acceptable present. Would a piece of superfine linen made into shirts at the Presentation Convent[39] in the neatest possible manner be such as your uncle would like, or shall I send him more Connemara stockings *of the best kind?*

August 13 — Garvey the gunsmith wishes very much to know if he and his brother could make a livelihood at his trade in your neighbourhood. He is nearly starving here.

August 14 — I went out yesterday to hunt to Ballymahon. The Boys, William, John Browne, Marcus and John Flynn, we were off at four, thought to be gone at three but the jaunting car for the Boys disappointed us. We went a mile below Ballymahon, found a hare, had a good hunt, three [*illegible*] when she vaulted. I dug her out, brought to Lough Inch in a basket, and after dinner let her out for the Boys and the *young hounds* only, when we had a great hunt which the Boys enjoyed very much. We had a good dinner dressed by Mr. and Mrs. Mahon and did not get home till nine o'clock at night. Frank told me there was a young otter in the island. It proved to be a rat and I had great work digging it out.

Send me a little of the best kind of tobacco seed by any opportunity that you can get. Tom Coy has the gardens of Ardfry. He has tobacco growing there but it [is a] very bad *kind.*

August 16 — Sally was very ill. We were sure it was a fever but it proved not and she is well. Morgan Connally's son, John Connally, a master of a ship, Mrs. Donnellan, Val Blake's Mother-in-law, Mat Barry's wife, Mr. Tighe of Newfield and many others died of the fever. Mr. Martin of Ross, two daughters of Robinson's, a son of Mrs. O'Brien's near Miss Gardiner's, Mr. Quinn with the one eye, a Mr. Flanagan, a friend and relation of the [Labarte?] family, was sent here as an assistant Commissioner General, had all a great escape of their lives and are recovered. Johnny Costello, Pat Joyce's sister, Mr. Daly's son of Dominick Street, Mr. Martin Deane, the Widow Persse, Mrs. Winston, James O'Flynn's sister, and many more are very ill with it. Indeed there are but very slight hopes about your Aunt Persse at her age, but before I close this letter you shall know all about her. There are 210 in the fever hospital and about 400 in and about the town in the fever. Poor little George Coates is in the hospital.

I before said that Sally was very ill. We at first thought it was fever but it turned out to be but simple indisposition and she is now well. Matty too has been ill, but not fever, and Jenny is very delicate these last few days but gone to Castle Lambert.

August 17 — Mr. [Tinsdale?] will make £7,000 of his seizure. I send you a plan of the vessel he took. I wish I could make a lot and I would not stop one day more in Galway. But no one sends anything in my way *tho* I have the name of being an easy kind of an officer. I have some hopes that I shall be promoted to be Surveyor of this, as Colonel Blake from his indisposition must be very soon superannuated. He cannot attend from his frequent illness. If that is the case I shall have £100 per year more, the better to enable me to lay by for you, or when I do retire, to have the greater allowance as my pension. I must never forget that I am to purchase a farm for you the moment you are out of your time, provided I learn that you are fit to be entrusted with such.

August 20 — I am happy you like a farming life. It would be the height of my ambition to retire from all care to the pleasure and luxuries of cultivating a farm. The greatest men in life have done so. It is not a lottery where like [*illegible*] a capital prize or a blank may be drawn, a nabob or a bankrupt, a golden chain or a wooden leg, but it is a certain, regular mode of life by which man raises his food with a pleasurable industry that mingles labour and enjoyment so perfectly and leads men to such healthful and virtuous pursuits that in all ages the peer and the peasant, the philosopher and the mechanic, have all fixed happiness to dwell in a rural life and to look upon its cares as the very essence of comfort and competence in this world. Read General Washington's letter to your Grandfather, study his life and you find him, after the most heroic actions upon the summit of military glory, the first patriot of his country, the advocate of Liberty, the successful asserter of the independence of America, reclining upon the peaceful recreations of a farming life, amidst the solitude of agricultural pursuits enjoying the delights of a country life.

August 24 — Yesterday morning, at half past four o'clock, your Aunt Persse died of the fever. She is most generally lamented. She has left Matty £150, Sally £50, and Frank £100, Miss Kitty Gardiner £200, Miss Carter £200, three of Captain French's sisters £100 each, and the Roxborough girls £100 each and Robby £50, and several other legacies. Now, My Boys, you may judge how the poor must be off when the rich fall a victim to fever. But I must explain. Great as her loss to the poor, the poor will benefit by her death. Let them pine in decay, jaundice, bile, dropsy, dysentery, sore legs, venereal, or in short any complaint but what is *contagious*, and there is no relief afforded to them. But to save the rich of fever that they might take from the poor, a fever hospital is built here, but no other is thought of. An infirmary for the cure of broken bones they think ridiculous, as the calamity is not contagious. Now it was the famine brought the fever, that is well known, and the one being coupled with the other, or following its heels is a blessing, for if it was the case that the people could die as in other cases without affecting the lives of the rich by contagion then they might rot unheeded and nothing would be done to save their lives.

You see now that out of an evil here good can be derived. But what a state it is, that an evil must be created to raise up a benefit in this unfortunate land or island. The people, it is now found, have been bled too copiously by the tax gatherers, and now the Government, through the medium of public works, are restoring a part of that blood into their veins. But how long this will last I cannot tell. But of this be assured, they must either discontinue the former or go on with the latter, else famine in the midst of plenty will again appear.

It is time I should stop for I have run my Boys a long race. No Tonabrucky hare ever kept up so long. But my pen cannot be taken from my Boys as it is the only mode I have of conversing with them. I beg to be remembered with kindness to Mr. and Mrs. Yates and family, Mr. and Mrs. and Miss Moore, in which all here join, and not forgetting your Uncle and Mr. Dore.

> Believe me, my Darling Boys,
> Your ever affectionate Father,
> H. S. Persse

I send this via Liverpool thorugh Dublin. Parsons never yet wrote to you. Although vessels sail constantly from Dublin, he would not inform me when any is about to sail. So I now employ Mr. Burton Newenham to forward for me this parcel to Liverpool. I fear I cannot write to your Uncle this time. Tell him all friends in Cork as usual.[40] No change since my last. James Morris not come yet. No letter yet from you since 25 July.

August 25 — The widow Persse's funeral has just set off for her family vault near that of all the Persses at Killeen Church near Roxborough. I remained here on account of Matty's illness although she is much better this morning.

[A fragmentary accompanying letter, addressed from Dominick Street, Galway, probably from a family governess or nurse, also survives. While corroborating HSP's account of famine and fever and in the region, it reflects a largely unquestioning acceptance of the 'unprecedented calamity', and little personal engagement with the distress of the 'lower orders' who have 'infested' the streets of Galway in search of help. In contrast to HSP's jaundiced view of the value of English relief efforts, the unnamed correspondent praises these 'liberal exertions' fulsomely. The following passage occurs in this letter.]

24 August — Since you left this country we have experienced nothing but misery, wretchedness and famine. The unpropitious rains of last year doomed thousands of our peasantry to suffer privations of the most afflicting nature. Numberless and melancholy are the spectacles of famine which have been seen throughout the country and particularly in this town. Groups of famishing paupers infested every street imploring sustenance. By the great and liberal exertions of the English nation, for which Irishmen will ever bear grateful recollection, considerable assistance was afforded, and indeed it may be truly said that without this aid Ireland would be in a deplorable state. We have now an abundant harvest, yet the effects of the famine are still great. We are now visited by a dreadful fever. Our hospital, though considerably enlarged by temporary accommodations, is not capable of containing half the number of patients claiming admission. There are at present 200 and upwards there in fever and men, women and children in several houses in town are also infected. You must conclude that from so much fever we must have some death to lament. Indeed the mortality has been great among the lower orders and some of our acquaintances have not been spared.

Letter 7

[Instead of following his usual incremental journal-style form, the majority of this letter seems to have been written at a single sitting, giving HSP's denunciations of contemporary Ireland a more polished rhetorical quality. Once again, his principal targets are the idleness endemic in the Ascendancy class, the evils of 'preference' and 'interest', and the sapping effects of overtaxation on those who might otherwise benefit from their own initiative.]

[November 1822]

[first two pages missing]

Captain French used to spend much of his time turning at a lathe, and made many useful and ornamental articles in his amusement. Here, indeed, there is a prohibition to a young lad practising his genius *on wood*, for the duty alone upon a ton of timber (that is 40 feet of 12 inch square) would amount to the price of a ton of wheat. Only think of a Farmer here, spending his whole time ploughing, manuring, sowing, weeding, reaping, stacking, threshing, and after paying rent, tythe, and taxes, if he requires a ton of timber for the use of his buildings, must not only pay for the original value of the timber, but also his whole ton of wheat (which now sells for £4. 4s. 0d.) for the tax or duty of one ton of timber, or one stone weight of tobacco, or 12 gallons of whisky. Here, my boys, is what makes the Farmers of this country not only poor, but miserable, and when you compare how much of the various necessaries of life you can get in America for your ton of wheat, *without* the payment of rent, tythe and other taxes, you will be able to see the cause that our people are worse a thousand times over than slaves, and that your Farmers are better off than our *Esquires*.

I should like to know when Frank and Burton are to go to you. You now know at what ages the Yankee lads are put to work, and you know whether you ought to be put sooner to the plow or not than you had been, and you also know whether the boys would do themselves more good *now* in America or in the nursery with Mr. Morris. I feel very anxious to learn about the 'three months schooling in the year,' and to see its effects in the improvement of the writing and spelling, in the letters you will hereafter send me. Let me have a full account of the mode of tuition, whether Lancasterian or otherwise. Your cattle shows and agricultural meetings, premiums, etc. always attract my attention. Any newspapers having an account of these in them would be to me a great treat, and I can get your letters and papers free now as ever, as the Earl of Rosse is still a Postmaster General, *but without salary.* Send everything to Richard Sadleir to whom I write how he is to forward them to me free of postage.[41]

The County of Cork is again disturbed as is part of Limerick, Tipperary, Kilkenny, and Clare. When was it otherwise? And when will it be that the rat which is squeezed in the dog's mouth to the point of death, will not bite and turn upon his destroyer, although he knows that his doing so only hastens his own destruction. I need not tell you my Boys the causes of these disquietudes. You know why it is that the men of rank and property barricade their houses, and travel with guards and firearms in this country, and do not in yours. You know why they are obliged to have armed men around their haggards, to prevent their being set fire to, why their cattle are houghed and themselves murdered.

Mr. James Morris is here. He says America is a very bad country, that the people have neither friendship [n]or hospitality, and that if I was there I would change my opinion of it altogether. I made him no answer, but I shall not change my opinion of America till I hear that an Insurrection Act is passed there which shall subject men to banishment for life for being out of their houses either before sunrise or after sunset, till a ton of wheat or a score of fat ewes can only sell for the *tax* upon a ton of timber, or *that* upon a *stone* of tobacco or 4 and ½ gallons of brandy. I will not change my opinion, till I hear a Judge tell a Jury that they know the law better than he does, till superior talent and virtue be a crime, and hereditary ignorance possess as of right all the roads to profit and emolument, till I hear that the dirt under your feet is more valued than the sweat of man's brow, till starvation shall take place in the midst of the *curse* of overproduction and superabundance, till I see the faro table, the mess room, the staff, the brothel, the Navy and the kennel sending up their members to be the spiritual pastors of the *Church of Christ*, till I see the tenth of every man's labour given to such ministers to enable them to live in luxury in foreign voluptuousness, wallowing in the champagne of Paris or the *Lachrimae Christi* of Naples (that is the tears of Christ, a favourite red wine drink of the clergy there), till I hear that the duty upon a barrel of oats, if turned into whisky, comes to eight times as much as the unfortunate Farmer shall get for the oats itself, till truth shall be a crime and punishable as a libel, till no man can keep a dog or a gun without a *licence* and *tax*, till the Law Courts shall so regulate taxation as to have a certain amount affixed for every word written, and no more than six to be inserted in one line, or twelve lines in a page, under a penalty of £100 per page, till I hear that what the Farmer shall take to market to sell is when sold to be divided between the landlord, the Proctor (of tythes), and the tax gatherer, leaving him to live in a house to which the entrance is in through the chimney, the bed straw, the food potatoes and water, the covering rags, with the pig for an inmate to share of the same food and same bed. When I hear that virtuous industry is a mark of disgrace, and hereditary indolence the climax of superiority and honour and boasted pride, till plenty shall cause famine, and famine fever, Bishops go to bed with soldiers and Prime Ministers cut their throats,[42] then and not till then will I give up my opinion of America, notwithstanding the declarations of Mr. John Burke, and Mr. James Morris and their safe arrival back to Galway, the former to work for his landlord at five pence per day, and the latter to walk the streets without any visible mode of occupation and employment.

My Dear Boys, you should learn much from this last circumstance. You see what an inroad upon industrious pursuits is created by a previous habit of indolence. Men accustomed to roam about gossiping, standing at shop doors, or at four corners, when they get into the world of occupancy and industry, are like so many fish out of water. They wonder that people do not give up their pursuits and stop to feed their apathy with some lie or wonderful exaggeration. The apprehension that you three might be innoculated with this Irish contagion, and that you would sicken hereafter at the thought of an active, industrious life urged me to remove you from the dire effects of such example, well knowing from experience myself that my happiest days were those wherein I was most actively engaged. And seeing that this country held out *no hope* of your doing good here, I hastened you off to the land where four corner chat is not the custom and where labour, whether of the body or of the mind, is the true representative of wealth, and not land.

Your Uncle Robert stays mostly at Newcastle, and not one of his children with him. Dudley is to get the property next year, and as his Uncle, Mr. Thomas Wade, is to be agent, I hope that something may be done to get the family out of embarrassments.[43] But I should be sorry indeed that I had not better expectations from each and any one of you than his Father can have of him. Think of forty thousand pounds that Dudley must undertake to pay, besides an annuity to his Father and a portion for his Brothers and Sisters. Think of his having the names of a fine fortune and place, but so encumbered as to make him but a mere agent to collect the money, to pay interest money, annuities, etc. etc.

Robert Parsons Persse is accumulating fast. He is still single and it would appear that he seems bent upon that life. Strange whim to be gathering up riches without contemplating who is to scatter them. Your brother Robert I rather think supposes himself an intended favourite, but Robert of Castleboy I look upon to be the best liar of the two and for my part I would not give him a tenpenny bit or as you would say a *cent* for his chances, for if he intended him for his heir he would have given him an education, and thus rendered him worthy of such consideration. Poor William still remains unheeded. He has nothing, nor ever will, I fear, for he is only fit to fill some sinecure place, and these are not now to be had. Henry fills his Post Office [position] badly, as he has saved nothing by living at my table free. He must now get a place for himself and learn to know the value of a dinner, etc. Matty is recovering fast at Castle Lambert from her late escape of fever. Sally will go with Mary Moore to Dublin on a visit. Your Mother [is] in excellent health but very uneasy about Dudley, for fear he is in the fever at New York, and this idea becomes more and more fixed in her mind because we have not had a letter from you these two months, and you, each of you, can figure to yourself her anxiety when no letter arrives. Tommy is grown quite fat at Castle Lambert where he has been for two months. Frank is grown very large and strong. He is the picture of *rude* health, and indeed Burty, too, is grown stout. I long to have the two latter with you. Miss Sadleir is in tolerable health, asks often after her poor *Dicky*. And Miss Geary, the pet of all the pets, that all the house, even your Mother, makes a pet of, is quite well.

I will not venture my pen at any length about this prodigy of nature, the child that we took off the street, that was left to die with four more opposite our house. In three weeks though not having a word of English and but three and a half years old, [she] learned to speak English as well as she did Irish before. She is without doubt the most wonderful and the most entertaining brat I ever saw. Only think of her dining tete a tete with Mr. Daly opposite, and keeping him in chat the whole evening, and that she learned to sing *Hop She*, Killkenny Theatricals, and various other songs, and her *small* letters she learned in one day. Not a word does she speak but with a very sweet accent, and her countenance, her body, and her hands, are used to give weight and intelligence to her expressions. She sings as true as the piano is played, and always upon the same key. She is cleanly to a nicety, and is now fast losing the effects of starvation. I tell you she is a great pet of your Mother's, and whatever your Mother desires she never forgets and never acts contrary. I never saw that gentleman's child that has such pretty manners and in my life I never saw any so far removed from civilization as all her brothers and sisters. Her eldest brother I gave a candle to light to. He asked me in Irish which [sister?] he was to put in the fire to light. And this Polly Geary is the Child that the aristocracy would fain make us believe was a *different species* of the human race, 'papist devils that nothing could civilize or amend'. Oh Ireland! what a country you would be today if you were governed, my Dear Boys, in the way you know I would wish. Many a Madame *De Stael* now among the Slieve [Rue?] and Tonabrucky children.[44]

I have had a great pain in my head occasionally which nothing removes but Lough Inch or a Clydagh trot[45] through the mountains with the dogs, but as Colonel Blake is still sick and the collector constantly away I very seldom can go out for I never go out on Sundays now, as I hear you are so strict in America. I wonder you can have any religion there. No tythes!!! No Bishops of Clogher, no laws to prevent free-thinking books being wrote or printed!! Church and State not united. Oh Wirra Sthrue.

We kept Dicky's day and we will, please God, celebrate the 11th November with full business. The C[?] we know nothing. The house is deserted and Mrs. C. and her [*illegible*] are on their travels for the improvement of their manners. The son and heir was very ill and very near following his dada with the gentleman's complaint. Mrs. B[?] is to be pitied, without child, settlement, or jointure. She lives alone as her husband is in the madhouse. The Whistlers and Burkes very well but Tommy Whistler has had his arm broke. Watty Blakeney has made off God knows where. His conduct was so bad on board the Pl[?] that he was turned out. James and John are most excellent lads. Doctor Blake sold his furniture and intended to reside in Dublin but he has been persuaded to remain in this town and is now fitting up his house anew. Pat Joyce's sister recovered [from] the fever, and now it is almost wholly vanished out of the town. My sister Mrs. Newenham is very ill. She has been in Dublin for some months about law business. Her husband and his family are still in France. She has now moved down to Portumna where William Newenham has a small lodge where they reside. Mrs. Farrell says he has succeeded in recovering a large farm for them, but I have heard this so often that I must see them in possession before I will believe it, and I must also hear that they are not in distress to be convinced that they are receiving the money out of it. Bobby *Molly* is very ill with the fever at Roxborough. I dare say you think how uneasy I am about him.

Your Uncle Burton Persse is still very stout and well, takes his hunt on fine days. I am not sure you know that he lives in a cottage upon the desmesne of Roxborough that was built by Regan the Priest. Born in the house of Roxborough, he went first to live at college, then to Persse Lodge, next to Tally Ho Lodge, after that to Loughrea, and now to this cottage at Roxborough. Upon being asked why he wandered about so, he said, 'I am like the hare, I was started at Roxborough, I ran my ring, and now I am coming home to die where I was first started.' Now, Mr. Sportsman Theo, was not that a good saying for the old huntsman to make.

Irish Farmers Misery

I sent Robert to the market on Saturday last to buy me two horseloads of potatoes and one horseload of hay and he bought the three loads for 5 shillings and 4 pence, 1 shilling 10 pence per load for the potatoes and 1 shilling 8 pence for the hay. The three horseloads would not pay for the duty of one gallon of corn whiskey, and would not buy one pound weight of tobacco, nor would they pay for one deal plank. Here are three men and three horses that came twelve miles to sell this produce for 5 shillings and 4 pence. I ask you now, would you like to be Irish Farmers upon such terms as these, and I ask you what could these creatures bring home out of the 5 shillings and 4 pence after feeding themselves and their horses. Never forget this picture of Ireland whenever the thought of your anxiety for her awakens in your mind, and do not forget a fat ewe for ten ounces of tobacco, aye *ten ounces*, and that ewe three years old, and the tobacco Kentucky leaf!

November 5th 1822 — No letter yet. Your Mother [is] very uneasy and indeed I do not wonder at her. She hears of my writing every day, but none in reply. Dudley in the yellow fever at New York is all her cry. She is almost sure of it. Pray do not be so irregular in future. I have frequently spoken at the house and told them that I was writing but I fear you will not hear from anyone but me.

The Widow Persse's Will is defective. Captain French will not act as the executor and all now is left upon Miss Carter. Sir Robert Staples had no tenure of his place (Spiddal) but [during] Mick Regan's life, and as he is dead Sir Robert must give up that place. See what work the fever created.

Burton Lambert, Captain Pat Burke, one of the Mahons and Burke of Tyaquin that has the palette of his mouth down are all appointed High Constables at £150 per year to keep the peace under the Preservation Bill. I wish poor William had been upon the list, but all the soldiers cannot be officers and this ought to confirm you in the wisdom that invited and directed your being sent to America, for you might grow grey before you would get anything to do here.

I now conclude, my Dear Boys, again soliciting you to persevere in the path you are walking in. Continue, my Dearest Children, to send me new proofs of your intentions to increase my happiness by a just devotion to your employer's business, to the end that you may establish such a character for yourselves as will in any case ensure you a comfortable livelihood and reflect no small degree of credit to the manner in which I brought you up. Be of good cheer. You already feel that habit makes your burdens fit you lighter. You have fine example before you. You see those that are industrious and frugal are ten thousand times happier than those in this Country who priding in the insolence of their birth have not in the whole range of their dominion over men and land not half the comforts or luxuries of an American Farmer. I feel I could scribble to you forever, but I depend upon my favourite Boys, the Boys that never caused me one moment's uneasiness, and that I expect will make the evening of my life, calm, composed, and happy, for I have nothing here to look to. My Daughters, you would say! Aye but can I look at them with pleasure and see no prospect here of their being wives or mothers, for no one marries *now* unless he has a great fortune to get with a wife to prop up some tottering estate. It's no match here made by the dictates of nature and reason. No. It is a curious thing made up part family connection, money, politics, and traffic, and the less they know of housekeeping, the genteeler they are reckoned.

Remember me with your best feelings to your good natured Uncle, to whom I write via Belfast. Assure him of my regards. Present my compliments to all around you, and be assured, my Dearest Boys, of the love and regard of your ever fond and affectionate, Father,

Henry S. Persse
Galway November 7 1822

I long for the Spring when I shall hear from you direct by the ships that will be coming here this next season from New York. I shall send you rams and ewes by every vessel that leaves this.

November 8 1822 — I got up very early to send my packages off, and the first thing I saw was Frank and Burton cleaning out the asses stable and having a barrow taking away the dung. That will do, says I, thank God you were not born natural lively with deformed backs. You will, my Lads, yet have your own horses to take care of, please God, in America. I am to get a car made for them and they are to do wonders for me. William is just come home from Connemara. He says there are large parts of that country that Mass has not been heard in for three years and as to a Church, that is out of the question.

Letter 8

Galway January 14 1823

My Dearest Boys,

Our uneasiness is at last removed by the happy accounts we have had from you all dated in October and early November, two letters from Dudley and one each from Theophilus and Richard. This great delay has quite deranged my plan of correspondence but I will pull up for lost time now that I know that my boys are happy and well.

If I was happy before at the step I took in sending you away from this misruled land what must my gratification be now when I see nothing but misery all around me, the Landlords without rents (God be praised) and the tenantry beggared, the same taxes and only a quarter of the money that used to be in circulation now afloat. Lands are thrown up and the Farmers broke. Even Tom Mulkere that bred the ram and ewe and that was worth 16 or £18,000 a few years ago is in jail. No man has a penny but the fundholders, and the tax eaters, and they do not know the moment that they will be dismissed. Oh, if you were to see the flocks of poor people that are now in the frost, and absolutely naked, and walking about in search of covering, and wages lowered to six pence per day in the town and 4 pence in the country and very little employment.

We were greatly pleased with the Bear hunt, but we had hoped that Dudley would have killed the fellow. I think I see Richard plowing, his arms quite stiff, his mouth going in as if he was eating something hot, but Theophilus dashing on like an expert coachman. No matter Dick, persevere and you will exceed the dashers. But, Dick, you should have read Theophilus's letter, and helped him in plowing through pen and ink, as he helps you through clay and sods. Read over his letters in future and mend his spelling before he sends his letters away. I hope this remark will not deter Theophilus from writing, for I like his style very much.

Robert Lambert was with us at Christmas. He only left us a day or two back. He is most anxious to join you, but I believe his father could not raise £5 to fit him out. No wonder. Mr. Lambert had fifty acres of wheat this year. If he wants a ton of iron, he must give two tons of wheat to pay the *duty* of the iron, one ton of wheat to pay the tax or duty upon one ton of timber, one hundred weight of wheat to pay the tax upon one deal plank or a pound of tea, five hundred weight of wheat to pay for the *duty* upon one hundred weight of sugar. He gives four hundred weight of wool where his father gave but one, to pay the duty on wine, and he will now get but one gallon of whiskey at a grocery store for a fat sheep. If he or his tenants want *tobacco* they must give a good ewe for to pay the duty upon one pound of tobacco, or fifty-two stone of potatoes, or ten stone of oats, or ten horse loads of turf. If he wants ropes for his farm use, he must give two hundred weight of wheat for the tax upon one hundred of hemp, nine hundred weight of wheat for the tax upon his servant man, twelve hundred weight of wheat for a licence to shoot upon his own land, and three hundred weight for every dog he keeps per year. If he should think it necessary for the *health* of his family to have a little French brandy in his house, he must give more than the price of two hundred weight of wheat for the *duty* upon one gallon of brandy. If I were to go into a detail of the stamp duties and show you how in the Courts of Law writings can have only so many words in each line and every page only so many lines under terrible penalties in order to have the more stamps — and to call a court where this practice exists a court of equity or law! In short, as I said before, taxes are a substantive, for everything *here* that we can *see*, *feel*, *touch*, or *understand is taxed*, and now, my Dear Boys, do you wonder that Mr. Lambert, although having an estate in this country, should be without five pounds to send out his son to you?

But it is not to draw your attention to the hardship of *his* case that I stated it, but to show in clearer colours the advantages you possess. If you, my Dear Boys, were Farmers in this country, how would you like to be cultivating wheat and paying rent and tythes and giving the produce of your labour in wheat or other stock to pay taxes? Do you now see that while such impositions exist here that no prospect could be open for your industry to gain by, and therefore I am not at all suprised that you thank God to be away from Ireland's misery and woes.

I forgot to say that Mr. Lambert paid forty-one guineas this year for his tythes at Castle Lambert, exclusive of what his tenants and himself paid for other denominations of land. So the more you think of these things I trust the more contented you will be. But see what a tax I paid lately. Parsons is bound to Mr. Warren the Attorney in Dublin and I paid for *stamps* alone £115 British Sterling for *liberty* to bind him to an Attorney. That much money would buy a fine piece of land, I dare say, in the States, but here I must give it for *liberty* or *leave* of the *Crown* to permit my son to exercise the calling of an Attorney's apprentice. But I will disgust you no more with this hateful Subject, for its effects create such terrible misfortunes, and these before my eyes every day, that I cannot work them from my mind.

Your Mother is better than I have seen her for years. She comes down regular, and goes to Church. I do believe that this little charity child which she is so fond of tends greatly to assist her health and spirits. She keeps always about her and by her odd and agreeable chat pleases your mother very much. I gave you a short history of this child before, but now she is so refined in manners, so correct in speech, makes so graceful a courtesy, sings so many songs, and with a strong and sweet voice, and as true as music could dictate, sings also the Church Psalms, repeats Hymns and speeches and is really such a prodigy that vast numbers come to the house to see her. She is not bashful. She chats at once to all and even goes over to Mr. Daly and dines with him tete a tete, and he is quite delighted with her company. She sleeps with Matty and is her child, but your mother *when I am not by* is fondest of her. In my life I never saw such a child. Mr. Morris has made a song for her which she sings and he is as fond of her as anyone else. She knows all about you all. Well, she says, Mr. Dudley is the mistress' own pet. Mr. Richard, Miss Sadleir's pet, and Theophilus mine. She asks hundreds of questions about Miss Matilda and constantly wants to know who Miss Persse loves most, Polly Geary or Miss M.P.S[adleir], about which she and Matty have very often a laughing fight. Matty said the other day she would get her [American?] child to her house. Polly said that she would send to Connemara for a child for herself. Each had a fight whose child should be best dressed. Anything Matty said Polly exceeded, but when she was hard run she said she would give her child a blue veil and put rings on her thumbs.

William is now at Abbert. He is still unemployed. He was here for the last four months. Henry had been very ill but is now quite well. Matty was returned to her health complete at Castle Lambert. Sally is very stout and I hope will soon go to Dublin on a visit to the Miss Moores. Robert at Castleboy with *his Cousins*, and has put on all the appearance of an old batchelor, wears knee preservers and cloth covers to the tops of his boots. He is only fit to be a driver over slaves. He would not for £500 a year spoil the shape of his nails by any unfashionable occupation.

Parsons here promises well, and I hope he will do. I expect to get him a suit about the legacies of your poor Aunt Persse, as there is some delay about the payment of these. Captain French behaved very badly about them. He was appointed the executor and he will not act as he has all her money in his hands. There is a political Bible Society man for you. Little did your aunt think that he would refuse to pay poor Simple for her coffin to this day, and neglect all her affairs and allow law to interpose to enforce her last wishes. Miss Carter is in possession of everything and I believe a great hypocrite or worse.

I hope we shall have a vessel here this year from New York, that I may send you more sheep and other things. As the ram, ewe, and lamb got so safe, it encourages me to increase your flock. Mr. Sadleir writes me that he sent up the rape seed to you. It is most valuable and will I know stand your climate well, so give it every chance. Sow some in June, July, and August also, and see how it will hold the next spring, and whatever period answers best, sow always at that.

The boys are very well. Tommy was delicate but Castle Lambert restored him. Frank is as hardy as a Laplander. I must soon send him to you. Judge Vandeleur never was able to go Circuit, so John Lambert got no salary yet.

I congratulate you upon the success of Mr. Yates as Governor of New York.[46] What relation is he to *Everett*? He has got a troublesome situation and not an enviable one, if he is not gifted with rare and transcendent abilities, such as Clinton certainly possessed. To my mind he is a man that has the capacity to turn great talents to the consideration and promotion of practical benefits and not by sophistical argument to lead the mind astray. It is easy to see into the clear stream, but here our statesmen puddle theirs to make it appear deep *as if* sense lay in obscurity.

The money sent here from London has repaired the bog road. A carriage may now go to Tonabrucky and to the [Bogoniers?]. Mr. Mahon, his wife, and son had the fever, also a young one that I know not whether male or female. You may judge what a pest they must be to me, and what misery they must have gone through. We everyday feel the loss of poor Tom Leonard at the Post Office. He was really a faithful poor creature.

A new misfortune now affects this Land of misrule. The Nation is split into open and undisguised religious parties. The Orange men aimed a blow and sought the destruction of [the] Lord Lieutenant at the Theatre because he was inimical to those soul degrading epithets and emblems which have so constantly and so disgustingly been aimed at the Catholic body.[47] This subject fills every mind. Every newpaper is taken up with it, and what is it after all? Three words of a wholesome law would put it to rest forever, as Dean Swift said about the 150 skins of parchment to his Mother's marriage settlement that 'she might lie in [in] Dublin as she pleased or not', for in those days a clause about such used to be put in marriage articles about having a house in Dublin, for it was not fashionable to lie in in the country then! God be praised you are away from all religious bickering and wars, and where your loyalty to your country is not built upon your dislike to your brother in Christ. People here go one hundred miles to debate upon the subject, fight duels and spend fortunes to attain their religious party views.

I have long wished that you would give me a peep into your household affairs. I have no idea of the kind of house Mr. Yates has, how furnished, whether his land is meadow or woods, what your system of living, how many in family, their ages, names, number of farm servants, lands in cultivation, stock, tillage, etc. Could you not say Mr. Everett Yates is ___ years of age, of an industrious, active turn of mind, neat in his person, regular in his farm arrangements has ___ cows, ___ bullocks, ___ horses, ___ acres of orchard capable of yeilding ___ hogsheads of cider fats, ___ hogs yearly, sells ___ and uses the rest, ___ acres of wheat, ___ barley, ___ rye. Indian Corn pays ___ $ per year state tax. His House is ___ stories high, has ___ parlours, ___ bed chambers. We rise at ___ o'clock, Breakfast at ___ o'clock, *and so on*, telling us, a winter breakfast of what composed, of spring, summer, and fall meals, that is, what fare at *each* meal generally in these seasons and how many meals and what drink?

Unless we can learn all this from you we never can be at home with you, as I know not even the name of Mr. Yates's place, and there are thousands who think he is not so well off as was Paddy Maley, and therefore you must give us some description of your fare, and residence, and your occupation. It is imagined, too, that the appearance of the country around you is wilderness with as few people as on the [Bogonier?] mountain, that you have no neighbours and of course no society except wild animals. Remove all this prejudice (as you write) by degrees. The climate too is spoken of as if it were a frightful one, that snow covers the earth and makes life detestable all the time it lays upon the ground, and your government such as bandits and mobs appoint, without principle or security. All this is set going to prevent people going to you, or taking your example, and the ignorant swallow it as true.

The Mayor's family will quit Dominick Street at March. So shall I, if I can get a house to please me. Mrs. Burke was pleased at your last letters. She is warmly an advocate for America. Mr. and Mrs. Reilly also take a great interest about you all. Pat Joyce asks every day about you and keeps the newspapers for you.

I was at Shantalla on Sunday. I sat with Mrs. Keogh chatting about you. She showed me T. B. P[ersse] on the wall that Theophilus put there as directions about his stockings that she was making. Her son, the next to John, as big as me almost, is a carpenter's apprentice, will be out of his time in two years and then he goes off positively to your side [of] the water. He is a good scholar, a good workman, correct merchant, and a very handsome man.

I kept Marcus Tonabrucky alive this year. He had the fever, so had the mother. I brought them through. Tom is always speaking of Theophilus and inquiring for him. He is almost naked, poor creature. Your Uncle Robert is very bad with his gout at Roxborough. No wonder, he drinks so hard, his knee is swelled up very large. Lord Clanricarde was there in a party shooting this winter and killed a great deal of woodcocks. We had severe frost and snow. The mail coaches could not travel for some days. We were afraid of another famine, that the frost would get at the potatoes and then the poor would surely die.

Sheriff Smyth was about to have an Orange Lodge here, but he was prevented. Had he succeeded, this town would be deluged in blood between Catholic and Protestant. How do you get on in America without these lodges? I send you a fine parcel of newspapers. I send them via Belfast by the John Dickinson, a constant trader.

Great changes in the Customs Department. The Board of Commissioners are dismissed and Captain French is now living in Ballinasloe, and he is no longer Secretary. I wish I had retired two years ago. Colonel Blake's estate sold for £10,250. His son joined him, and that will not pay his debts, so he and his whole family are all beggared, and not knowing how to do anything and no hope of a place out of the taxes. I know not what will become of his fine boys that were bred up with such high notions. All the estates will go, for the taxes take all the rents, and the people that have money due to them are calling in the principal as they can get no interest. They will take no excuse, but sell the estates to pay themselves their money, regardless what it sells for, and thus are the Landlords ruined.

As there will be plenty of opportunities now offering I will hasten this letter to a conclusion and I leave out all small news for the young folk to write about. I warned them every day that I was making up my parcel, but in vain. I see no one sending me a letter to forward to you yet.

And now, my Darling Boys, adieu for the present. Let me entreat that you persevere in the good work of your own improvement. Let the industrious example before your eyes strike deep in your minds. Let the comfort, the happiness, and, above all, the peace and harmony, which reigns in the truly free country you are placed in, quiet every uneasiness that your absence from me might create, but ever recollect that no uneasiness could be equal to that which the dread of seeing you at home without industry, the excitement to industry, or even the common competence that nature demands for your support. Think of the numerous families that are now in these countries bred up with the *highest* expectations and that have not even hope to rest upon. Think of all this, Darling Boys. Think what uneasiness, what anguish I should suffer were I to have you to look at here, and not be able to rescue you from the snares of Vice which idleness is weaving every day for those who are unemployed. Think again, I say, my Dearest Boys, the children whose virtuous prospects my heart receives such comfort from, think of the pride I take in your manly determination to be independent of the smiles or the frowns of the great, proudly confiding in the resources of your own energies for that competence which the fair hand of Nature offers to Man all over the globe, where tyranny and oppression interposes not to withold from him new blessings, and in a voice of blasphemy says that the cause of distress is the superabundance of food.

I could write you forever, but I have run to the last moment (January 29th 1823) and the vessel is to sail the second of February from Belfast. Excuse me to your Uncle. To him I will write by another opportunity, and I hope to mark my sense of the obligation I owe him by a nice present by the [next] vessel from this.

Let me know when I am to send Frank out. I shall send you two ewes this year if I get conveyance for them. I am glad Cobbett's *Gardener* was liked. I shall send you Tull's *Husbandry* which Mr. C[obbett] praises so much.

I have not seen an American newspaper this many a day. Pat Joyce gives me a good many for you, and always asks for you. These I send. I have a great notion to take Sloper's House above West Lodge, for the town does not agree with me. James O'Hara is to be married to the Bishop of Tuam's daughter, that is Captain French's niece.

All join in love to you, your Uncle Mr. and Mrs. John Sadleir, and Miss Matilda, etc. etc. and believe me, my ever Darling Boys, your very fond and affectionate Father,

Henry S. Persse

January 30 1823
frost and snow gone

Letter 9

[In this letter HSP meditates further on questions of nature versus nurture, again holding up Polly Geary as an example of how environmental factors may determine educational and social accomplishment. His assertion that humans are 'creatures of circumstance' is, as in previous letters, a view that he uses both to critique the class-bound atrophy of Irish society and to emphasise the advantages his sons now enjoy by being in America.]

Galway March 26 1823

My Dear Dudley,

It is always a great pleasure for me to hear from you, but I cannot tell you what gratification I feel at the receipt of your affectionate, manly, and sensible letter. Affectionate, because it breathes love and devotion to your Parents; manliness, because you show a true pride in putting on a determination to become a useful and industrious man in society in order to make yourself independent of all men's frowns or favours; and sensible because it expresses these sentiments and reads a fine moral lesson to your good little brother Tommy.

I never wished to force you to any particular profession in life, but there are a few that I would protest against. I would not make you a soldier of fortune to be the slave or the sport of tyrants. I would not [make] you draw a sword in favour of the French government in order to aid them in dictating a rule of internal regulations for Spain, but if I were a Spaniard and that France dared to place a hostile foot upon my native land, if I had but one son, or had I an heir dual, I would denounce that son that would even hesitate in flying to stop the enemies bullets. So much for my opinions about war and soldiers. You have chosen to be a merchant, and you begin like one who would intend to do well. If you purpose to raise up a wall to a great height, your foundation must be good, the work close and well laid, the progress slow that all may settle regularly. The rule, the line, the square, and the plum[b] must be used, otherwise the greater the mass that is put together the sooner it tumbles and carries destruction. Just so in mercantile affairs. If the line and the *rule* are not attended to, if the foundation which your present pursuit ought to be your object to attain, if system and regularity are not practised in all the proceedings, if too much haste is sought for to gain the summit, all will be chaos, and that chaos will end in ruin and destruction.

I have not been an idle observer in life, and I have often remarked that most of those who set out in life with large capital and those *high* notions which always attach to money, that they seldom succeed, while those who begin as you are now commencing, and purpose to climb the ladder step by step, not seeking to miss one of its rungs, always get on and never can be without the means of support. For when they find it unprofitable to act for their own account, they are sure to get employed by others when character does not desert them. I dare say that you must see the truth of what I say around you, for I could name fifty in Cork who are now in affluence and that commenced clerks, for *one* that began as gentleman with capital and that was successful. The clerk sees into everything. The books which he keeps show him how money is made, and how it is lost, and having learned the value of money in early life by working hard to obtain it, he keeps his earnings and spends nothing but what is really essential and of this he even keeps an account of so as to know how it was spent. And when capital falls into his hands as he advances in life, either by his own acquirement or the assistance of his friends, he is sure to put it to a proper use and to guard it with that prudence that teaches him to protect his most vital part.

I am glad you like Mr. Anderson, for as you are but the creature of circumstances, which children all over the globe are, you will partake in spite of you, or I should say imperceptibly, of his methods and manners. If he is a sloven in his affairs, keeps no books, leaving anything to chance and irregularity, you will contract the same habits. But if he is, as I find Scotchmen generally to be, frugal, industrious, sturdy, and systematic in all their dealings, then it must be entirely your own fault if you do not, when leaving him, go into the world with the fairest prospects and the best of characters. And I ask you, Dudley, where will you find in America *such a person*, having his health, in want of anything that a reasonable man could desire?

I mentioned 'the creature of circumstances'. This I will explain to you. I mean that had you been born in China, although the child of your present parents, that such is the force and effect of example that you must be to all intents and purposes a Chinese in language, manners, custom, and religion, provided you had been sent away from your parents the moment you were born. For man being an imitative animal adopts the forms and customs in which he sees those around him brought up in, like Miss Polly Geary who now (though born in Connemara) speaks English most correctly and sings with the piano as correct as possible, but had she been left in her native cabin would have been almost as ignorant as the pig, her former inmate. You may therefore be assured that it is nearly a truism that man may be judged of by the company he keeps and that he forms his character from the circumstances that he is associated with.

I do not think the proverb of the rolling stone gathering no moss applicable to you. It is only to those who roll themselves about that it would fasten on, and this seems to be your only and first move. You hitherto proceeded from the impulse of filial duty. You obeyed my wishes, and now you make [your] choice in the field I put you into.

And, having made that selection without the least constraint, it is to be hoped, nay it is most confidently expected, that you will apply so assiduously to that pursuit that nothing will swerve you from your object. You know that in America no one will deal with you or favour you on account of your name or your relations, that all is a clear stage before you, and that according to your tact and talent you will be allowed to perform the part of Hamlet or the gravedigger, whichever you are found fitted to act. In your own hands are therefore your own fate. Apply, study, gain the ability to reach the top of the wheel, and there is no law human or *divine* in force in *America* that can stop you from taking the palm. That you are young enough, there is no question. Lord Erskine was a midshipman at thirty-two and went *then* to study the law, and rose himself up in spite of the aristocracy to be Lord High Chancellor of England. I hope now, my Dear Boy, I need say no more to you, for I have so good an opinion of your disposition that I rest satisfied you will push yourself forward and be in my old age my pride and my consolation.

March 27 — Since I wrote you the above, your letter dated Febuary has come to hand and I shall observe your *private* communication, and by a vessel that sailed the tenth of March from New York and now daily expected I shall send you 25 guineas as you desire, to buy a suit of Yankee built clothes. But now to business, as we say when play time is over. Why do you not let us know upon what terms you are fixed with Mr. Anderson, and why not detail to us what line of business Mr. Anderson is in, what articles he buys and sells? For merely to say you are in a store would leave us to guess whether it was a kelp, a herring, or a turf store. Write me like a merchant and tell me what you sell to the country, and what payment you give them, if part cash and part barter? Say what kind of country produce you take and where you find a market for it afterwards, and what freight you pay to New York or where you send it to. And also say is your house doing well? Is your employer well paid for his *trouble*? Is there great rivalship in his trade? Does his neighbour grudge him? What good he is doing? How many houses in Paterston? And what inhabitants? Is the country around you thickly settled and are they in as good circumstances as those on the road to Mr. Mahons of Ballymahon, otherwise Mahonville of [Bogoniers?] Town.[48]

Now suppose you were of age, and that you understood your business as well as your employer. What do you think would be a decent or moderate capital for you to begin with and how much of that capital will you be able to acquire by your own earnings between eighteen and twenty-one?

The County of Cork is in a state approximating to open rebellion, the Insurrection Act is in force there and I see by the papers that numbers are hung and transported without Judge or Jury. To be out after sunset, to have a charge of gunpowder, a pistol, flint, bullet mould, or anything like or appertaining to firearms is sufficient to convict any person. There are a great many young men, nay the whole of the sons of the estated men of this kingdom, now soliciting and praying, aye!, and making all the interest possible to get to be *Constables* in the police to be employed in taking up, committing, and punishing these unfortunate people, these truly oppressed and distressed and heartbroken white slaves. And they call it *pride* to seek for their livelihood in this line and that it would be degrading to till the earth or keep a store, and they delight in the distractions of the country in the hope, as they cannot find occupation in war *abroad*, they may in wars and rebellions at *home*.

All your desires about Tommy shall be attended to. I purpose to send him for a little time to Mr. Moore's office to smarten him! He shall write you and his Uncle, and he writes well. Send your letters always to Richard Sadleir by hand and I leave him directions how to forward them to me free. Write me often and give me all your *Mercantile News*. We daily expect a vessel to the Burkes from New York by which returning I shall send sheep, etc. etc. etc. and newpapers. She sailed, I hear, the tenth of March. John Kelly is going to send out a vessel to New York with a cargo, and his brother goes on her to purchase a return of tobacco and staves so that we shall have a fine opportunity back for anything I want. *Send me a small* quantity of tobacco seed, a half ounce at a time.

Matty writes you all the little news, so I say nothing *in that way*, and as I write so very illegibly and as I wish this letter to be placed before you in the *clearest* manner, I desire Mr. Morris to copy it out fair that you may the better be able to peruse its sentiments. I need not remind you of your duty to Mr. Anderson. My former and first letter of advice contains all that was necessary upon that subject and I pray you as you love me to follow its precepts for it was dictated from the very core of my heart.

I could write to you forever but I must stop, for the vessel that is to take this is to sail shortly from Limerick. You must communicate with Richard and Theophilus who I regret to say write us but seldom. I hope they are well and with love to you and them and my best respects to Mr. and Mrs. Anderson,

Believe me, my Dearest Dudley, to be your ever fond and
affectionate Father,
Henry S. Persse

Colonel Blake is absent for the last twelve months and the Collector very seldom here, so I have frequently the whole concern upon my back. If I do not write as often as you expect, recollect that I write *more* than all those who have nothing to do. I sent on the thirtieth of January a letter of thirty-eight pages directed to you *three*, My Boys. I wrote a very long letter to your Uncle all about you the other day and he will tell you of my anxiety for your advancement.

Letter 10

Galway, June 6, 1824

My Darling Boys,

I would write you separate letters but that I am so engaged with Tommy's departure, and the Customs House regulations keep me so close in attendance.

I now write by your darling *little* Brother who is a most excellent Boy, esteemed by all who know him. His mind has been bent so earnestly upon joining you that it was in vain to delay his departure. He took such a liking to the master of the Governor Tom[p]kins that I let him go. His outfit is pretty good. He has a fine three masted ship under him, and I have supplied him with the means to go to you to pay you a visit although New York I purpose to be his station. There he may be of use to you all by and bye, as a friend in the city is what everyone in the country should have.

Charles Lambert accompanies Tommy, and I would hope that a good place can be found for him as he is really a good lad, not at all of the disposition of the lad that cries about Athenry, and therefore I am very anxious that he should be well placed.

We have had the most

[*pages missing*]

must admit under our system, it was good policy in the Roman Catholics of old to devise the plan they did for the young high bloods, than to leave them loose upon society to demoralize the community around them.

The Customs House and Tommy's voyage keeps me so hurried that really I do not know what I write, and there are so many about Tommy taking leave that he does not know what he is doing. Never did any little fellow carry with him more regrets and more the esteem of his acquaintance than Tommy, so that I have every hope that he will be a credit to the Perssonian Society in Montgomery County.

I could not get anything to send you as a present that I could wish, so I send you three gold brooches enclosed in this letter with one for Tommy.

The vessel just about to sail, so, my Darling Boys, I pray you every happiness and success, as I am, my Dearest Children,

> your ever fond and affectionate Father,
> H. S. Persse

There are specimens of Mr. Holmes's writing sent out. He is a most correct young man but cannot earn a bit of meat for food!!!

Letter 11 (to DeWitt Clinton)

[*HSP sent this letter, his fourth and most significant to DeWitt Clinton, via his sons. It was not delivered in timely fashion, and in Letter 12 HSP bemoans their delay. When it finally reached Clinton, its contents were no longer immediately topical, since protectionist legislation had been passed in the interim. For Clinton's position during the tariff debates see Introduction, pp. 51–53. It is unclear whether Clinton replied.*]

Galway

June 4th 1824

Sir,

[*In two opening paragraphs, HSP evokes former correspondence with Clinton and portrays himself as a non-partisan commentator on the tarrif question.*]

I look upon the opposition to the Tariff Bill to be nearly allied to that bigotry which interdicts the exercise of human reason. A people boasting of independence pretending to despise the joint efforts of that unholy band who overturned and laid prostrate the most powerful Republic that ever appeared on the face of the earth, and that may when they gather strength unite to destroy you. A people I say holding threat to this sleeping Lion who are obliged to be dependent upon these very nations for wherewithal to cover their nakedness, but then there is the favourite [*illegible*] 'let us have our workshops in Europe'. Fine talk. It reminds me of the Dandies in this Island who say 'let us have our fashions from London, a London built coat fits so well 'pon honour'. Fine talk for those butterflies of the day who care no more for country than country cares for them. They and many like them draw all the means they can from this wretched place, and send it to London to fatten the Lords and jobbers there and enable them to enslave us. But this is not the conduct I would expect from 'Yankee' people, men free of thought, and independent minds. 'Workshops in Europe' might be relished in some degree if Europe said 'Granaries in America', but were it even so, and it is the very reverse, I would be for protecting manufactures because your liberty and independence are connected with them. Read the Life of Washington and see how the fate of the war hung suspended upon the thread of a blanket. Were you not near being slaves for want of supplies for your armies? Are the powder mills and founderies included in the 'workshops of Europe'? If they are not, why are shoes, coating, shirting etc? Are they less essential to the fate and success of an army than powder and ball? Can an army in America fight without coats, hats, shoes, shirts, blankets and tents? Oh, but says some Anti-Tariff man, 'when the war comes we can make these things at home when we cannot import them'. Thank you, Sir, you will encourage the manufacturers during war, and the return you make to them who enabled your armies and fleets to be victorious and yourselves free is to open your ports to the *canaille* of Europe, who, feeding upon potatoes and water, lodged and housed worse than the Pig of America, are enabled to manufacture cheaper than the easy laughing, full-bellied, well-housed and well-clad American![49] Am I to suppose that you wish your manufacturers to be as poor as the European ones? Are there to be no manufacturers in America until a race of feudal Lords take possession with the aid of an 'Established Church' of the whole soil of the Republic and rendering it sterile by monopoly deal out to the operative classes so miserable a stipend that they shall be reckoned the cheapest working and the worst fed people on the face of the earth? Will you protect the tillers of your soil from being [*illegible*] by the productions raised by the hands of these ill-fed and half starved multitudes and give no protection to artisans and manufacturers at home? Is this equality? Are the agriculturalists who are forced by tyranny to flee their native lands and seek an asylum in the United States entitled to every protection upon arrival, and will the manufacturers be told there is none for him? That he must go back like the felon 'to the prison from whence he came'? Is it because the Wool Lords, the Iron Lords and the Cotton Lords of Europe make slaves of their working people that a nation of free and enlightened men know not how to give employment for fear of making slaves also? Have not the tyrants of Europe serfs? Have they not worse than slaves cultivating their lands? And why does not the fear of such example deter the free American from putting a hoe to the ground? Are not potatoes and water the sole food of the great bulk of the Irish people? And why do not you prevent the cultivation of the former lest they may be applied to the same purpose in America as they are here? Are you become a nation of Chinese? Must all live by raising the products of the earth because their forefathers did nothing else? Can men be said to be free where the effects of a bad and short-sighted policy aided by foreign tyranny and oppression interdicts and circumscribes the occupation of man? Is taste nothing? And are all to be agriculturalists because a bad policy says so? May not one man make an useful citizen as a manufacturer who would not thrive as an agriculturalist? Shall the doors of America be open to the world and those of the whole earth only conditionally so, or restricted towards her?

The Governments of Europe detest and abhor that of America beyond apprehension. Do they not exclude you from their *Holy* Compact and look upon you as a spurious and an illegitimate offspring, an upstart that sets such an example as to convulse all their subjects and keep them in eternal commotion? Would they stop at any expense of blood and treasure to rid the world of your 'successful example of democratical rebellion'? May they not annoy you yet and succeed by uniting all their forces to subdue you? Would they not find in Hartford a Convention to join them?[50] And how many other places may there not be conventions in, as well as that of Hartford? Would the experiment do you any good even if you were successful at war? You are a nation without revenue, for war stops your Customs duties. Would it not be wise to keep the powers of Europe in awe and fence up all your weak points by showing an inpenetrable front, flank and rear? But how can this be done while you are dependent on those who long, who sigh for your destruction, for that which is to cover your nakedness? Away with the delusion. To be free you must nowadays be strong, for power is right, and that power you cannot have if you are dependent. A penny *kept* at home is more profitable than two pence brought from abroad. What use in all those valuable vegetable and mineral productions which the exploring your country now unfolds? Are they too to lie dormant and not to be applied to the purposes for which Nature designed them?

Would you not work such mines as those of Mexico and Peru because they were slaves that did so under the rule of the despots of Old Spain? Are your Canals to be solely employed in the conveyance of the [*illegible*] stuffs and lumber of one town to another? And are those articles which belong to manufactures never to move on its waters and repay its cost? Would you buy from the Algerines if they 'sold cheap' and that your doing so would strengthen them and *their system* and enable them to fit out ten ships of war for one they are now capable of doing? To use a vulgar phrase, would not this be buying a Rod to whip yourselves?

But you will say 'Oh! our foreign trade will be destroyed, our shipping deserted if we have not woollen cloth, buttons and calicoes to bring back from Liverpool.' This I deny. The alteration in the tariffs could not cause a sudden change in your imports. It would be some years before you would be able to supply yourselves, and during that time your population increasing, your imports would continue still considerable. But would not manufactures open new employment for your shipping (Does not the coasting trade of coals in Great Britain give more employment and rear more hardy sons for the Navy than *all her* foreign trade put together)? And what would be the effect upon your inland seas and canals? Would not manufactures increase considerably the employment upon these waters with less risk and more profit than any other trade? Would it not be more advantageous to your nation to have your vessels repaired and the freights [*illegible*] upon the Ohio or the Lakes than at the Thames or the Mediterranean? And ought it not be more pleasing to the eye of an American to see a cargo of salt, coals or iron coming down the canal and manufactures returning than any trade that could take place between Liverpool or Stockholm? Yes, yes, 'But we have no surplus or unemployed population' you will say, 'our people find plenty to do and what need we more.' Events and circumstances deny this position. Besides your Farmers are not paid cost for raising produce. There are times and hands for manufactures when and for whom agriculture does not find occupation. If you did want people for such calling! millions in Europe would flee with their capital and industry and settle in the States. They went there before, after the peace, but their services would not be accepted. That golden hour was lost. It is a shameful blot and gives the lie to your boasted protection to the oppressed and distressed of all nations. They were obliged to flee your soil for they were of the proscribed class. But if ever you were scarce of hands to employ in manufactures, is there not a substitute? One that Europe under the old and tottering *regime* dare not make use of. Are there not saving-labour machinery which her starving people will not permit *her* to use, and against which no prejudice reigns with you? Might not these machines be greatly extended and their powers improved in a country where their value would be appreciated and their usefulness unfolded? And with such in the hands of American enterprise and skill, how small the portion of human labour necessary to cover the shame of a highminded and free people and enable them to clothe themselves without the aid of their legitimate enemies. Is the power of steam to be only employed in propelling boats or ships at sea, or would it be commercial sacrilege to convert its influence to any other purpose? Are there no mill [seats?] yet unemployed? Have your rivers ceased to run their course? Do they not possess power to manufacture for the whole world? And are they to be doomed to unoccupancy lest the feelings of a trading adventurer should be wounded?

For my part, I do believe and I do speak from my long practical experience that if there were not a single woollen or cotton manufacturer in the United States, that if a protecting law were to take place that more persons would leave Europe in seven years to engage in these branched than with the assistance of power-machinery would make a sufficient supply for your whole population, and that in 20 years you would rival *Old England*.

But I am told that 'Europe will not deal with America or purchase her products if America does not take her manufactures in return.' Facts are against this reasoning. What is it that any nation takes from another out of pure gratitude or reciprocal sensibility? Holland takes nothing from Ireland. Nay, she undersells our staple manufacture and rivals us in distant markets. Still, we import her flax seed because it is better quality than that of the United States, though the latter takes our linens in exchange. There needs no further illustrations. The tea of China finds its way everywhere, not in exchange for other products, but because it cannot be got so good and cheap elsewhere. And the wines of France in the days of her determination to overthrow all the aristocracies of Europe were never in more profusion upon the tables of the titled than at that very period. Away, then, with the nonsense of national reciprocities and gratitude. In trade, all people seek the best and cheapest when they are compelled to go abroad. Three thousand per cent duty upon American Tobacco cannot stay the Irish peasant from seeking for it as his greatest enjoyment and comfort, and to prefer it even beyond his food in the house of famine. The [*illegible*] from which links our system together and enables our rulers to pay the troops that keep the multitude from rebellion. You are alarmed about your cotton. Be you sure that whenever it can be had elsewhere *cheaper*, that we buy no more from you. South America and the East Indies may do that very soon. The latter has made a rapid advance in that way, so manufacture your own I say, and then you are prepared for the worst. When the day comes that you are rivaled by the East, you would no doubt to fulfil the favourite maxim, buy there, and in your pilgrimage for cheap goods annihilate the cotton planters and the manufacturers altogether. If Mexico can sell wheat at a less price than Pennsylvania and New York, why should the millers of either State be bound to lay out their money at home but be permitted to send abroad to 'buy the cheapest'? Need I go further to prove the fallacy of that doctrine upon which your political economists build their arguments? Protection and your free institutions have turned your wilderness into a garden. Grant the former to the capitalist and handicraftsman, and your Union and independence stand fearless of the whole world.

I know it is said that 'you are yet too young a people to have manufacturers to clothe yourselves'. That argument was made use of previous to the last war by those who sought to induce you to bear insult and wrong without seeking for redress, yet you youthfully moved upon the waters with your litte 'fir built' barks, and with your juvenile inexperience you humbled the greatest mistress of the ocean.[51] [*Four long sentences here flatter Clinton by evoking the Erie Canal as an example of American enterprise.*] And now can I believe that there is yet in the United States a rational feeling that the nation is too young to dress itself? After the race of glory and the arts which it has won by distancing all Europe, shall I be told that a people whose institutions are not half a century old yet, who have taken the palm from the greatest naval power that history can speak of, that has done more in the art of inland navigation in a few years than an equal number of centuries could boast of in the Old World? Am I to be told that they must be clothed by foreign hands, that they are too feeble to put on the garb of their own manufacture? It was as confidently said that man was unfit for self-government, but America has solved the problem and I 'guess' that it would be now as difficult to make a true born American believe to the contrary as it would be to make a Newtonian think that the world was in shape like a trencher.

A little more and I am done. To let you have one practical illustration of what has stared me in the face since I was able to think, in the province in which I reside in, Connacht, we have no manufactures. Agriculture engages all, and although we boast of the density of our population, we have hundreds of thousands of acres of fine improvable lands in a state of nature, wholly unprofitable, yet misery and starvation are around us, and that too in a state that no pencil could paint, no pen describe, for nothing but a view of the original can give a true picture. We pay no direct tax, lands are cheaper let than in other places, but we export agricultural produce to England where it is admitted free and we take back manufactures in return, which pay no duty. Here is what the anti-Tariff people would seek for, but what are the effects? The pictures I drew your attention to before, best bespeaks. We are destitute of capital, England absorbs all, and we are miserable beyond expression. But this is not the case in other parts of Ireland. In the province of Ulster 'the manufacturer is placed by the side of the agriculturalist' and there we behold a race of hardy, clean, well-fed, educated people, able to pay higher rent for the same quality lands, and enjoying a portion of comfort not at all known in any part of the agricultural counties of this Island.[52] In *Ulster* the manufacture of linen and cotton is carried on extensively and connected with agriculture. At some periods of the year the weaver is found in the fields, at others the Farmer is in the loom, and thus the measure of employment is best fitted up. But what is most remarkable, and what ought to be studiously noticed by your people, is that a few years ago (in my own time and recollection) the Irish Parliament protected by heavy duties the infant manufactures of Ireland from the overwhelming rapacity of England, and now that the manufacturers are instructed in the art, these duties are withdrawn and a free intercourse established between the two countries. The manufacturer of Ulster (or the North) who is 'placed by the side of the agriculturalist' exports his cotton webs to Manchester, where he is well remunerated for his industry after paying the expenses of freight, insurance and other charges. We paid a high price during the early years of instruction and protection for our clothing, but as competition and skill increased we found the article getting every year cheaper and cheaper till at length we were able to undersell the *British* even at their own doors. Nations, like individuals, must make sacrifices. America must serve her apprenticeship to manufactures, and while her sons are in a state of probation they must be protected. But let them be out of their time, and I doubt not they will soon teach the Old World the good effects which a free and cheap government have upon the arts, sciences and manufactures, and that they are not to be rivalled by the slaves of any nation in the world. With this case so analagous to yours I close my remarks by asking was this 'fostering one class at the expense of another'?

As every lover of humanity is deeply interested in the prosperity, independence and happiness of the United States, I sincerely hope that its people may steer the best course to attain those ends, and that you, Sir, may long live to aid them in the pursuit with your patriotic zeal and transcendent abilities, is the constant wish of, Sir,

> With the highest consideration of respect,
> Your very obedient and humble servant,
> Henry Stratford Persse

Letter 12

> [*In a characteristically elastic manner, HSP in this letter shrugs off bad news that*
> *Theophilus had been cheated by his employer and moves swiftly to entrepreneur-*
> *ial thoughts of how his sons might most sucessfully invest in land. His news of*
> *family deaths and misfortunes — such as the bankruptcy of the Lamberts and*
> *the humiliating return of his nephew Henry Persse — are used as a backdrop to*
> *suggest, once again, how fortunate his sons are in having escaped Ireland.*]

[Galway, Ireland

January 1825]

My Dear Richard and Theophilus,

On Christmas Eve we received letters from you, Dudley, and *Thomas*
and no better Christmas box did I ever get. To be sure, the bad treat-
ment to Theo was a drawback, but what in life runs smooth without
meeting some obstacle to ruffle its surface? Thank God he was not tied
to him, and I am sure that any magistrate would make Mr. Yates pay up
his agreement, to which end I will write your Uncle.[53]

I hope my Dear Boys got the £10 British which I [sent] in November
last, as I was uneasy that your pockets were empty. I have got a little
gathering of wearables to send you by Mr. Kelly. They are coarse home
spun for your farm work, and I would not send finery because I wish to
be represented most in your hours of industry, and my hope is that these
things will be used in earning for you the means to buy superfine. Be
assured I have not forgotten you. I already remitted to London £100
British. I will send £100 more in a few days, and the further sum of £100
I hope also to send you timely for your purchase of a farm this coming
spring, as there is nothing I have my heart so fondly set upon as that of
having you both fixed upon a bit of land called your own.

I agree fully in the idea of your going *west*. Everything in my mind
depends upon the first step you take, and, as you are loose, young, single fellows, a new country is the place for you, where *time* as well as
your own industry will be working for you. For you may be assured

those back counties will soon be all filled up and according as they are, the property becomes more and more valuable. Besides, the climate, in my mind, should operate to induce you to move back. Do not fear to do so. The momentary want of society or neighbourhood will be but of short duration, for these lands must fill fast in consequence of the [Erie] canal, and then you will be amply repaid for your first privations. I was looking at the map. I see Ontario County lays well. The lake and the canal gives it many advantages, but Monroe County looks better to me upon *paper*. The Great river that runs through it and over which the Canal passes at Rochester above where it empties itself into the lake must make *Monroe* County a desirable spot. Upon a good river is a good place, a mill seat is a good thing, and a river makes plenty and gives many advantages in a warm and dry climate. The *Genesee*, too, seems a very large river, rising as it does in Pennsylvania. But any opinion of mine can be only superficial, but my idea is you should move to new, good, and cheap lands, a good position, well watered, and a mild climate. All other things may follow as population increases, but if those advantages do not exist, nothing can *bring* them to you. You may gather people together by art, but good soil, water, and climate would be a difficult task indeed! Look, therefore, to natural and local advantages in the place you are about to pitch your tent, for a good selection may tend greatly to your future advantage. And do you not be uneasy on my account, for when I can pay you a visit I would not stop were you to move to the Yellow Stone river or the banks of the Pacific Ocean. When Dean Dudley Persse purchased Roxborough for a trifle he was called a mad man to quit Dublin and go to the *wilds* of Connacht among wolves and other wild beasts that *then* frequented this part of Ireland, but he had in his view the future interests of his family and was wise. Would that I could like the Dean or you go *west* for the future benefit of my children, and I would not hesitate by distance.

My thoughts are all absorbed about your future welfare. Sorry am I [that] I did not think earlier this way, but minds that are young only think of the present. So it is my duty *now*, from experience, to tell you what considerations you should have, which if you do not embrace you will regret when you grow up with a family about you. You will regret it, remember what I say. Dean Persse's estate went farther west, for his son, Colonel Henry Persse, purchased the estate of New Castle for £300 and it would now let for £2,000 per year at the least if out of lease. But why should I make use of any illustrations to you who are in a country which knows only of improvement and increase, and where property is every day becoming of more and more value?

I like very much your account of the husking parties. They are rational and profitable sources of amusement, far surpassing our barbarous assemblages called wakes. Any little detail which opens to our view your customs and manners is most acceptable. It is but the just results of free and good government that you are governed so well and so cheaply, and you have defined it in a few words most satisfactorily when you say you [are] rich over the mind and us over the body. I think we shall never loose our bloody and martial code till the *paper* [money] system falls, and it hangs only upon the good opinion, peace, and dominion of the moment. The least reverse and all crumbles. It is not like anything else. In nature there are some signs before dissolution, something to notify the approach of either a sudden or expected decay, but in the paper money system it is all rude healthy manhood or sudden death. Today it is invaluable, to doubt its virtue would be to become the laughing stock of society. But the next moment and the wonder is how anyone could place their hopes and their means on filthy rags. Mark therefore its career, and you will see it vanish in the manner I state.

Is it not extraordinary that wheat at *Dover is* seven shillings and eight pence per quarter while at *Calais* in France, fifteen miles distant, it is but three shillings and five pence? Show anything to equal this!! The cause is that in France wheat is bought with *gold* but in England with *paper*. Now only suppose our system to be invaded with French wheat or American tobacco. Why, our whole national paper debt would not be worth the rags it sprang from, for leaf tobacco is six shillings per pound!!!

I am very glad that De Witt Clinton is elected. He is a noble character and a pure magistrate. But why is it that Tommy never gave him my *long* letter upon the tariff? I am quite fretted that none of my late letters got to his hands after all the trouble I took to write them.

You will learn with regret the death of our friend Mr. Lambert. Castle Lambert, his house, was always open to my family. I wonder will that coxcomb Charles *now* lay his mind to industry and not be like his brother Robert, bred up to be a strolling idler. The sum he is left, £350, would be of use *in America*, but *here* it would not keep him in Windsor soap and blacking. His brother Parsons works like a [sailor?] to gather rent for a landlord, tythes for a proctor, and money for tax gatherers, and in all probablility an ejectment will close *his* labours, when he will have the heart rending picture of misery staring him in the face. Richard is to be a Doctor, but when will he get a fee? And what is to support him till then? What pains of mind must he suffer before he can get to earn the price of a breakfast? Let Mr. Charles [Lambert] study these things and reflect upon what is before him here if he is mad enough to return (*home* I was going to say, but that he has not in this country). I can tell him Castle Lambert is shut against him *now* as close as Roxborough is against your cousins by Dudley their brother. Watt will let no one stop at Castle Lambert that he does not specially invite, and when Lady C., Betsey and Anna Maria go there they must pay for their diet as at an inn.[54] Robert got the turnout there and must now seek shelter from his brother Burton who is in Kerry.

January 30, 1825 — I have been so worked at the Customs House with this new system and English officers that I could attend to nothing but the *Customs House*. Only think that the Tidewaiter must brush the metal weights and adjust them, and I must stand by to see the work done. I am now ten weeks discharging one cargo, and under the old system five days would have done it. The goods are *timber*, *deals*, and *iron*. They are weighed and measured as if they were bars of gold or pieces of 'Shittim Wood'.[55] The duty is now like that in an English Man of War quarter deck.

February 3rd 1825 — I now remit the £100 to London to John Kirwan and Sons, with directions that they shall accept your cousin Richard Sadleir's draft for that amount for you. And I fear, my Dear

Boys, that I shall be delayed longer in sending the other £100 I promised than I expected, for I am disappointed by events in getting it. So you must begin with this £200 and reckon on £100 per year besides, and perhaps the other £100 will come as a surprise upon you. But this I say, I will never sleep easy till I send it to you. I pride myself so much in the good conduct of my Boys that I feel myself largely their debtor.

Henry Persse is arrived.[56] Athenry is big with story, it would fill a volume to tell the lies he circulates. He worked his passage to Liverpool and made his way like a stray dog home and arrived just after the Sheriff had seized every pot, kettle, bed and moveable your poor Uncle had. Stranger yet, here your aunt was consoling herself to Miss Persse [at] Persse Lodge that Henry was not there and that she had heard he was doing well, when in he walked!! Your Aunt remained unmoved and speechless. She sat at one end of the room and he at the other. Not a word, no welcome, no kiss. His Father had fled to save his person, so if this fellow had any feeling what must he think at the embarrassment his return must have created? Where will he go? Not to me, I swear. To Roxborough, whence the Squire had turned [out] Fathers, Mothers, and Sisters? Castleboy perhaps? Ah! I need not tell you how close the gates are shut there. But then there is his Mother's family, the luxurious-living Wades of Fairfield, the great sheep Farmers. No. No. These people had *rent to* pay. Aye! and by this and taxes they are in the Sheriff's hands and every spoon, bed, chair, table, aye, and every tail upon the land is advertized by the Sheriff to be sold by auction, and old Guzelbelly Wade himself made off to hide his body from the jailer. So you see what Mr. Henry has to witness upon his arrival. But the blackguard will enlist (for they are recruiting at Athenry). He will be sent abroad and we shall never hear his name mentioned again.

Pray Mr. Charles Lambert Esquire read this and learn to do some good. Would you my pretty Mr. Charles Lazy like to add to such misery and increase by your incumberance the woes of your relatives by heaping yourself upon them in the midst of their distress? I tell you one thing, and your eldest brother desired me tell you so, that if you do come back, that your foot shall never be placed inside the gate of Castle Lambert. But what am I about, sure Henry says you are gone to South America, and that too to the most unhealthy spot in it from whence no European ever escaped death. Such is the Athenry story. But we do not believe *everything* we hear from that quarter. Just so the story he gives us of Miss Lansing and Richard to be married immediately, 'a pretty girl but the devil a cent has she'.

Now upon this subject I think I should say something, for I did hear this report before. If I were asked, I would say you are too young, Boy! and yet too poor to hang the cares of a family about you. I know nothing of Miss Lansing but by report, but I know this, that every account tells me that my Boy lives in the estimation of every industrious, sensible man about him, that he has hitherto been a Prisoner [*illegible*] to a fewer families and that if he has patience and extends his acquaintance, he may form a connection that may tend to assist his honest views and lay the foundation for a comfortable support for his future progeny. Richard is the eldest brother. He is the head of the Persse *aristocracy* in America. He must take care what he does, for if anything were to happen [to] me, I would leave his younger Brothers chargeable upon him. I think I heard that your cousin Richard Sadleir said when he was asked to marry that he had seven wives to provide for and these were his Brother's Daughters and that he could not marry 'till they were provided for. However I may think, it matters but little. While you have in your Uncle Sadleir so affectionate a parent, you will encourage no intimacies nor connections, you will do no act, without his advice. And in all things I pray and beseech you to be guided by him who is our most valued friend and has proved himself such by the kindest acts to you all. Besides, my Dear Boy, it is not affection for a woman to ally yourself to her at a period when you have not the means to support her. Nor is it right in her to heap upon you the cares of a family when you have so many others to contend against.

Far as I am away, I know my advice will be listened to, although there are those here who would not permit it to enter their hearts. Here is William, still a prey to drunkenness, even at my table in the family way, sometimes in the middle of the day, and sometimes brought home speechless and to all appearance dead. I know not what to do with him. He is not only an incumbrance to me but to himself. Yet this is the kind of man called a good fellow in this country, where drunkenness is considered an honourable virtue, and sobriety a sordid vice. To be sure, it must be so where men with feelings and dispositions like Mr. C. Lambert are bred up to do nothing and to kill time, as they call it, take a cheerful glass. No wonder then that this country should be overstocked with idlers and drunkards, and that I should be delighted at your being removed from the contagion. If we do not soon have a war to employ and take away the high notioned fry that swarm our streets I know not when the evil would stop, unless regimentals are invented to induce them to take on in the mechanical and other labourious arts, whereby the opprobrious term of tradesman would be annihilated. For instance, the Duke of Shavings, Count Sawdust, Lord Anvil, Sir John Hammer, Earl Plough, Viscount Harrowpin, Baron Drill, the Marquis of Shears, the Honorable Mr. Wheelwright, the Prince of Wagon Drivers, the Worshipful Mr. Weaver, His Grace of Tallow Chandlers, for instance. I say would not these nicknames, with the additions of gold and silver, lace boots, ruffled shirts, four square cocked hats, spurs on the toes, and rings through the nose, patchwork coats with epaulets, would not all this coax young lads to work? And surely their names would be more respectable and sound better than Lord of the Bed Chamber or Groom of the Stools. To make the thing complete we should not permit any tradesman to be one but the eldest son, the legitimate fruit, the first born, and make all the rest paupers or beggars and then you would see what Interest would be employed to get a young man made a tradesman of.

Your Cousin Eliza Persse is to be married in a few days to the largest man in Dublin, a Count White.[57] It is not a bad match, but she is exquisitely beautiful and if pains were taken the first man in the land would have sought for her.

A fine ship, the *Magnet* from Philadelphia with eight hundred hogsheads flax seed lost at the little island this side of the cliffs of Barna. She was bound here. We have no pilots here and any American meets misfortune in the Bay. I took the crew off the wreck at night at the risk of my life and the safety of theirs.

I am worn out. I must stop and so I ought, for I shall soon write again by the ships expected here with flax seed from New York. May God bless my Excellent Boys prays your affectionate Father,

H. S. Persse

I will send a good farm boy to you for seven years when you are at home on your own plot.

Galway February 4, 1825

Letter 13

[With the Erie Canal now fully operational, and the prospects good for economic development in upper New York State, HSP tried to fulfil his wish to help Theophilus buy a farm, sending the remainder of the monies he had promised in 1825. His reliance on Clement Sadleir, whom he had praised the year before as 'so affectionate a parent' to the boys, proved less than fortunate, however, and in the 'great blow' described below the money was misappropriated, either by Sadleir himself or by his sons and cousin. This unfortunate result apparently came as less of a surprise to the intended recipients than to HSP. In a letter of 5 April 1826, congratulating Theophilus on the news of 'the handsome present my Father has made you', Dudley had complained of Sadleir's dubious record in financial matters, cautioning him several times about how 'badly' Sadleir has treated some of their aquaintance and warning that it would likely be 'some time before you can realize the cash' from him. Shady dealings were evidently something of a Sadleir family trait, with one of Anne Sadleir Persse's more distant cousins, John Sadleir, later becoming one of the most notorious embezellers of the Victorian age (and the model for the character Mr. Merdle in Dickens's Little Dorrit*). After causing the failure of the Tipperary Bank in 1856, this Sadleir took his own life in dramatic fashion by swallowing prussic acid on Hampstead Heath. HSP's determination that the 'loss' should be amended was eventually answered, for in HSP's letter of March 1829 Sadleir is back in good grace, being referred to as 'your good Uncle'.*

HSP's mention of his letter of introduction to DeWitt Clinton belies his earlier claims that he did not wish his sons to profit from the kind of 'interest'

Clinton might be able to exert. The letter, however, was most likely not deliv-
ered, as no communications from HSP survive after 1824 in Clinton's well-doc-
umented archive.]

Galway
August 24 1826

My Dear Theophilus,

I wrote you a very long letter some time back and sent you a letter of introduction to the Governor, hoping he would introduce you to some respectable Proprietors in the West. Since then I find you had gone West before you got it. But I hope nevertheless you sent him my letter accompanied by one from yourself, in the writing of which I would hope Mr. O'Hara has helped you. It would be a great step to you and recommendation of you and advantage to your future prospects in life to be so highly introduced, for there are always doubts entertained about strangers and particularly Irish ones. I write this by Mr. Kelly, who goes by Liverpool and promises to see you before his return.

All our hopes about the money in New York is a dream. Instead of your Uncle and Cousin putting it to interest to accumulate, it has been squandered away. They say to the Boys, but do not say to who. I send you a copy of the letter I got from Sadleir, Ray and Co., and a more unsatisfactory one I never read. It is a great blow against you, but you must not despair. *Those who broke in upon that fund* shall rue the day they touched it, and my whole exertion shall be devoted to make you amends for the loss, as you had not hand in the spoil. But how could I expect S[adleir] R[ay] & Co to take care of my money when they could not do so with their own.

We certainly shall have a Famine here next year. The potatoes and oats have failed. The misery now is beyond description. Gangs of people go out at night to rob the potato fields, pulling up the stalks to take what potatoes they can get at in that way. I have suffered a great deal, they having robbed me [largely?].

Henry went off from this some time ago and never said goodbye to anyone. We hear now that he went to London to make interest to get out to Botany Bay, but that there are so many claimants that he could not get a promise and is coming back. I am told he now thinks of going to S. America where if he stops he must first learn Spanish before he can do any good. William is here without hope or expectation — an old man [in] every way. Parsons moves from one house to another and has given up Post Office and Attorneyship. I never open my lips to him, and I must tell you that Richard wished to stop here and fall exactly into their shoes. He would if he stopped, that I could easily see. Robert goes on correct and regular at the Post Office. It is a poor thing, but he will not overrun the emolument and thus he will be happy and respectable. Burton is as good a boy as lives, but Frank wild and idle. He is

[*remainder missing*]

Letter 14

Customs House Galway
January 18 1827

My Dear Theophilus,

Do not imagine that the lapse in my correspondence has been occasioned by any forgetfulness of you. No, my Dear Boy, it has not, for there is nothing in this life which so much occupies my thoughts as to have you settled to my satisfaction. But the fact is I wished to accompany my letter with a *Power of Attorney* to you to obtain the money I vested in Sadleir Ray and Co's hands, but strange to say that I have found it impossible to get it done. We have had no *Mayor*, *Sheriff*, *Recorder*, *Magistrate* or other corporate officer to put the Seal and Certificate to it as there were so many charges against the Corporation at Law that to evade the costs etc. there were no officers elected last August, but it was held out every day that there would be in a few days, and so I was held in suspension and hope, expecting every day to be able to get this trifle effected. Would you believe it that numbers of robbers, house-

breakers, coiners, etc. etc have been taken up, but that there was no
Magistrate to convict them to jail, so that rogues have had a holiday
time of it. I now send you the Power of Attorney enclosed, and hope it
may get safe to [your] hands. I regret to say that Mr. Sadleir has used
me badly. He has never to this day sent me an account of this money,
so that I do not know what was actually taken up or *who* drew it. I wish
you would get an order upon your Uncle W[illiam] B[lakeney] Persse
for the monies paid for Henry and I will try to get it for you.[58]

I did hope I could by this time be able to speak positively as to your
wishes but I yet feel that some months must elapse before I can do so.
I have some arrangements in contemplation which are not yet matured
sufficiently to enable me to speak as satisfactor[il]y as I could wish, but
should I succeed which I am fully inclined to expect, you may be sure
that my first desire will be to give you a good farm. I have been pressed
upon very much of late, the marriage of Matty, my living in N[?] for
nearly a year.[59] The return of Richard added to some monies I paid for
Parsons and some demands I never thought would be made upon me
have thrown me back a good deal. Otherwise I would have followed up
my plan of remitting for you 'till I had completed my wishes for you.

With respect particularly to your marriage, nothing would give me
greater happiness than to see my Children get into that state according as they arrive to the years that nature destined them for that state.
At [the] same time, there are many important considerations to be
taken into notice before a step of such paramount concern should be
decided upon. In the first place it, should be seen pretty clearly that
there was a full and warrantable expectation that you had not only the
means to support *her* but also yourself, for it could not be true affection in taking her hand to lead her to the abode of want. The next
thing for your most serious consideration is to make a proper choice.
Beauty of person is certainly attractive but soon vanishes and then
those of the mind and the disposition are estimated and approved of.
The value of a woman of sweet temper and industrious habits is ines-
timable as a partner in life. She is the greatest blessing God has given
to man in this world, but where there is not an union of sentiment,

and where domestic strife exists, what misfortunes follow, what misery is perpetuated.

When therefore, my Dear Boy, you shall have the means to support a wife, and meet with one such as I describe, you have always my consent to change your state. I have no opportunity of knowing anything of the one you have fixed your eye upon, but I doubt not but she has been well brought up under such worthy parents and would make you happy, but you must

[*remainder missing*]

Letter 15

Galway
June 2 1828

My Dear Theophilus,

I wrote a long letter to the Boys by William Kelly and desired them send you an extract, and to send you:

— seven linen shirts
— two striped callico, ditto
— six pair half stockings
— five cravats
— one cannister of snuff all marked and numbered for you. I also sent newspapers with the trial about Castleboy and desired you should get one.[60]

Now Mr. Kelly's departure was so unexpected and so sudden that we had no time to do anything, and his brother John was taken so much by surprise that he did not fix the credit for him in London to draw for the amount of the tobacco, so that William Kelly will I suppose be nearly a month in New York before he can draw for your money in favour of Dudley. This will be no great delay to you. It was all occasioned by a Mr. Richard Anderson of Richmond, son to the President of the U.S. Bank, who came here to see Kelly and was obliged to go off immediately yesterday in the coach at two o'clock and to be in Liverpool this evening so as to sail in the packet for New York.[61]

There will be a vessel leave this for New York latter end this month. By her I will send you the making of a handsome suit [of] clothes and two excellent dogs. Mr. Kelly assured me at parting he would not return this time without seeing you at your farm, and just after he went off I got a package of letters from Matty from Dublin, that followed Lord Rosse to London. I know you will now be happy to learn that Matty is quite well after being given over by the Doctors in Dublin. I hope Mr. [Morris?] approved my last production about manufactures. When you have a < . . . > send me a few of his papers < . . . > particularly if he insists that an < . . . >

I have everything < . . . > settling Burton at Havre < . . . > may learn to be a polished < . . . > of business and a complete < . . . > I would hope he may yet be of < . . . > use to his Brothers in New York < . . . > to him. At all events I < . . . > him the opportunity and < . . . > ever being a hanger-on upon his home relations, as I have too many of these kind of chaps to look at already. Indeed, I must say that none of you promised better at his age than he does, for he is even *here* a right good boy.

I wish your Brother would write you and give you all the small news, for now I must write *separately* to Dudley, Richard, Thomas and Frank, lest they may not know what things in the trunk are for each of them. I think you said there was some lady very attentive to you. If I can get your Mother to work a cap for her then she will have such an one as no money could buy in your State. I remain, my Dearest Theophilus, your ever fond and affectionate Father,

H. S. Persse

Perhaps you could send me some real Locust tree seed. I mean that kind of timber that never rots, and if you send any other seeds of good timber I will make Burton Persse sow them in Persse Lodge.

William just in the same way. I < . . . > him. Henry very seldom. He is < . . . > drinks too hard. Parsons doing < . . . > Robert in the

Post Office. Sally < . . . > Your mother very well, delighted < . . . >
Grand Children. Mr. Morris < . . . > steady good man, you always
< . . . > him.

Letter 16

Sea View, Galway
March 30th [1829]

My Dear Theophilus,

   The safe arrival here of my beloved child Thomas with his cargo of
flax seed after a very boisterous voyage has gladdened the hearts of us
all. He is really a fine little man, has made and is making many friends
for himself, and I hope will make some money too, for without some
of *that* men in this life are supposed to be neither industrious nor frugal, and hence but little respect is paid to them. Dudley's partnership
with Mr. [Campbell?] is another source of gratification, and Frank's
attention to his business not less so. I hope poor Richard will now get
on, and I hope Burton will emulate his Brother's good example, to
which you all should strongly advise him. He is the weakest reed and
requires support and advice as France was a bad school.

   Mary's letter to your Mother we were all greatly pleased with. Indeed,
the sentiments in it do both her head and heart great credit. By the return
of the vessel to New York your Mother will send her reply and I shall
send you some little matters. I purpose to send out Tommy Ward to you.
He is a boy that has been with me for four years, is an able working lad,
very sober and very willing. He shall be delivered to you free of any
charge to Johnstown, to work for you for his Board and some little matter besides for one year from the time he arrives. Billy will tell you what
a good boy he is. Perhaps he would take on with you when the year ends,
at all events he will be a great *help* to you and you will have him so cheap
and if you approve < . . . > I can send you one next year to work for his
board *only* for a year by my paying his passage. William is to send you by
Ward a beautiful dog. She is one of the handsomest I have seen.

I wrote you so long a letter a few weeks back that I have now nothing to add but my love to your excellent wife whom I hope is quite well.[62] Regards to Mr. and Mrs. Edwards. Do not forget me to your good Uncle and [Mrs. D?] and believe me, my Dear Theo, your ever affectionate

H. S. Persse

The trial about Mary Coffey and Mr. George [McConnell?] is over. Mary is proved to be correct but the trial separates Mr. and Mrs. M. The latter accused Mary of cohabiting with Mr. M. but she failed to prove the scandal. It is a very bad business as it has separated a hitherto happy couple. Parsons and Henry are in Cork. They went there to vote for Mr. Newenham at a very contested election.

Letter 17

Galway, October 4, 1829

My Dear Theophilus,

I was made very happy by the receipt of your and your wife's letters of July last, and I am glad that you and she liked the few things I sent you. I am sorry to say that what I sent by the Agnes that was castaway in the West Indies [is lost], that the merchant there kept all to himself, took the boxes out of the cabin and brought them up to his own house under pretence of selling them to pay the expense of the vessel, but really kept them all for his own use. So you suffer with all the rest. Thomas has been here for some months and we were all highly gratified with him, he is so amicable and his disposition and manners so captivating, I 'calculate' he will do well. I have sent you by him patterns of blue cloth, buttons, etc. for a coat and pantaloons. Your Mother sent you six large silver spoons and Matty sent some little matter also, all which I hope got safe 'ere this. I sent some cloth to all the other Boys.

I went to great expense about Burton. I sent Robert with him to France last year and now I have been obliged to take him away and meet Thomas in Liverpool, with whom he proceeds to New York on board the new American ship Hermitage. All this expense you can form no idea of. It has pressed me with other matters very much, so that it will be some time before I can send you anything till matters come round. I had Burton first at school for six months, then got him into Mr. Beckham's House where I paid £50 per year for his board. He and Mr. B. did not agree and he then went into Lafitte's House and boarded out at the rate of £75 per year. I found then that he was left to his own mercy, that France was no place for him, that in Havre he would be taught to smoke and drink and to gamble. So I made an [exertion?] and sent him to the country. I hope of steady habits. In fact, Theophilus, though I had a great object in view in fixing Burton in Havre, when I found what a demoralizing place it was and that he was not under the same roof with his employer, I determined at once to remove him from the contagion of dissipation and folly. The expense has been enormous but what is the inconvenience I feel to the heart rending sorrow I should suffer hereafter if he was to have fallen a victim to French vices and folly.

It is not to be supposed that I can be as good a judge at this distance of what is best for your interest as Mr. Edwards who lives on the spot, but at the same time, from all I have learned from persons who have visited Johnstown and Canandaigua, the latter bears the palm for a fixed residence.[63] The soil, the climate, and the prospects of advance are all in its favour, so that, unless it was at the express instance of your wife's family, I should request your leaving where you are.

I am sorry to tell you that Sally has made a very hasty match. She has married Mr. Creagh without the consent of her family or *his*, and the stipend they have to live upon is very slender at present. He is a near relation of Lord Rosse [*illegible*], one of our relatives. He was intended for the Church and was at Trinity College having a small salary from the Post Office for his support, but how he will now proceed I know not. A little patience might have

[*remainder missing, save for a note on the side of the last page:*]

I was glad to hear that Billy is a good boy. When Mrs. Morris sings the song she sets off to school. Larry is very well. So is the fox and the martins. Brandy was stole but Badger is well. Peeler is sick and lame. James Grogan and Thomas Ward, Mary Browne, Mary [Conroy?], and Winny desire to be remembered to Billy and expect a letter from him, as does Polly Geary.

Letter 18

Galway,
April 22 1830

My Dear Theophilus,

I wrote you by packet some time back informing you that I would send out Thomas Ward to you to work and assist you for one year. He is now the bearer of this letter and the terms I send him on are these —

I have paid his passage and gave him money to take him up from New York, in all £5. 0s. 0d. For my doing so he agrees to work for you for three shillings per week and his diet etc. for one year from the day he arrives at your house. He is a good lad, sober, steady, and hard working. I have a double motive in doing this, first to assist you, and next to save the lad himself, for I have a desire to advance him. If you find him useful you can agree for next year, and if not I could send you another boy next year that would gladly give his labour to you for twelve months for his diet only upon my paying his passage for him, which I will do if you desire it.[64]

By this opportunity I send you some things which I trust may be acceptable. The list is annexed, and I have given Ward particular directions that your share shall be kept safe when he is giving up the articles intended for *Richard*, *Dudley*, *Frank*, and *Burton*. I have sent Mary Anne a very handsome work box, fully furnished with all kind suited for a *good housekeeper* and as I 'calculate' that she has made me a grandfather by this time I send her a lot of baby clothes for the newcomer which I hope she may like.[65] Had I your measure I would have sent you the things ready made. I send six shirts made from my good linen. I had them made a size larger than Robert's, and I hope they will fit you. The cravats are the newest fashion, the Connemara socks and stockings the best to be had here. As you say you sometimes kill your own meat, I send you a butcher's knife and steel, and a bread knife to cut that article for *the children*. For Billy I send blue cloth for a jacket, calico to line his pantaloons which I send of corduroy in hopes that he may be a good boy, which if I learn he is I will not forget him. I wish he would *dictate* a letter home and give a full account of himself and how he is employed. Mary Anne could write it for him.

Dudley is always writing to me for the balance due by you to him of $112 and 38 cents. If the account is right you may draw in his favour on me for that amount or desire me to remit it to him, but in paying you what I remitted him for your account I do not see why I am brought in debtor. I gave Ward three new blankets, one quilt, two pair new coarse sheets, one pair of which is sowed up for a bed filled with straw. All these, tho' for his use to save you expense, are ultimately yours, and I expect he will deliver them in good clean condition to you. Coleman the ploughman from Persse Lodge accompanies him. He is a most excellent workman at all kinds of husbandry, sober as the president of a temperance society, and civil as a friend. He has a great attachment to our family and I would recommend Mr. Edwards or you to keep him for he is a faithful slave. His Father was a decent respectable Farmer till the system here harried him off the land in spite of the most exemplary industry and frugality. He is a man of all work, builds dry stone walls, makes collars

[*remainder missing*]

Letter 19

[This letter, addressed to Persse Lodge, Johnstown, is to Theophilus's wife.]

Sea View, Galway
August 1 1830

My Dear Mary Anne,

I take this opportunity to send you a few little things by my very particular friend Mr. Martin Veitch. They are scarce worth your acceptance, being only a small box [of] cotton, some thread and cotton lace
and four collars. They, however, will show you that I do not forget you.
I hope the things I sent you by Ward got safe and that you liked them.
I took some pains about the workbox and some credit for *my* plan of the
cloth cover for it. I hope Miss Anne likes her things. They were all chosen by *myself*.

Mrs. Persse would write to you by this opportunity but she is so
engaged with my daughter Sally who is expected to be confined any
moment and the doctor these two days in the house with her.

I long to hear from you and get a full account of how you are now
engaged in your domestic affairs. I hope William is a good boy and
makes himself both agreeable and serviceable to you, and that I shall
hear that Ward and Coleman conduct themselves satisfactorily. Thomas
is still here. He does not return till September when a cousin of mine,
Mr. Robert St. George, accompanies him, and, if you approve, he will
stop with Theophilus to learn the farming business. He will take out
with him bed and bedding so as that you should be at no expense to
provide him with such.

All my family are well and join with me in love to you, Theophilus
and Miss Anne,

and believe me to remain your very affectionate
Henry S. Persse

Letter 20

Sea View, Galway
November 27, 1830

My Dear Theophilus,

I write this for your information as well as that of the Boys in New York, whence I desire when they peruse it to forward it to you.

Thomas sailed on the eighteenth in The Francis and your Mother and I suffered dreadfully on that account as the next morning at about 3 or 4 a most dreadful hurricane commenced here with one of the highest tides ever known. It was not a spring tide yet it broke over the sea road from Master Ffrench's to Lord [Clanricarde's?] and made a perfect strand of it all and injured many houses, broke through [Invers?] marsh, leveled the whole bank, threw down all the walls, Folans, [Invers?], Hanlons, took the boats from the Recorder's Quay and some bathing boxes and left them at [the] villa on Mr. Daly's lawn, broke down the walls through [Boher Moyne?] filled all the houses there and at the [*illegible*] and went into Mr. [Shore's?] parlour, sending men women and children, pigs etc out through the tops of houses, destroying wheat and flour at Killeens and filling all the houses in Dominick Street eight feet deep. It took the Claddagh in the rear and here the scene was lamentable, everything in the houses carried away as the tide soon came in in the [front?]. Many were drowned and all the furniture swept away. The boats broke from their moorings and were carried across into the town beyond the Customs House and all the other streets. Two of the water guard drowned and poor *Rascal*, his crew and himself, lost boat and life. The water was up to Mrs. [Dea's?] door near the Four Corners. Turf, potatoes, and fish destroyed, and pigs innumerable drowned. The Connacht Journal tells you of the shipping. The [Provost?] is in a potato garden at Ring[?]. The ship *Blackenstone* is near [Murrough?] and will never be got off. Another vessel was dismasted in the dock and six others are greatly damaged. In Mr. Connor's [garden?] 40 sheep were drowned, many lives lost at Oranmore and Clarenbridge, and poor Mat St. George lost everything. The battlements of the bridge of [Oran?] were carried away and now the whole Claddagh are begging about the town having [nothing] to lay upon but the bare ground.

I wrote to Galena and Co, and he says there was no storm at Liverpool, that Thomas had a fine offing N[orth], and the next day and since a S.E. wind which continues, so that I 'calculate' that Thomas will have a good passage. Strange there was no storm even in Dublin. They were quite surprised when we wrote about it.

Times are very bad here. The bank will discount. They are afraid of a run for gold. They would discount a good estated man's note, he placing a Government debenture as a security against it. You will feel this by and bye in New York, for every article will fall as money gets scarce.

William Kelly is on his way [with] 350 hogsheads of tobacco and either 200 hogsheads of flax seed or 250 barrells flour to fill up. Mind that. What will you say if the flax seed comes here? It would be very hard to get a credit on London here from the bank, as the state of England alarms everyone.

Matty has got *another* daughter. She is quite well and so is young Burton.[66] Your mother was not at the [*illegible*] as she could not leave me, I was so helpless with a sore leg. The old Captain turned against James O'Hara and is secretary for Val Blake in an election petition to turn O'H out. Mrs. O'Hara wrote to your mother in great alarm about it and it is feared that V.B. will get in. But in or out is now little matter, for the game of plunder is almost destroyed. We

[*remainder missing*]

Letter 21

[*The year 1832 saw the outbreak of a major epidemic of cholera in Ireland, which claimed the life of HSP's son Henry in August. In Letter 22 HSP gives details of the wave of deaths that swept the Galway region. A Central Board of Health was established to attempt to prevent further outbreaks of the disease, and met with considerable success. The Board published daily reports giving the*

*number of new cases and deaths throughout the country. For the two-day period
of 25–26 August, for instance, 10 new cases and 6 deaths were reported in Galway city. Reporting for rural regions remained minimal. The figures HSP gives
in Letter 22, reporting 16 dead in a local village, are probably accurate, as his
general reference to '1000 took ill and 500 died' squares well with cumulative
totals for Galway, published in late August, of 1,178 cases and 546 dead.]*

Galway, September 5, 1832

My Dear Theophilus,

You are already aware of the death of my Dear Son, your Brother
Henry, who departed this life the twenty-fifth of last month. It has been
a sad blow to your Mother and me, but God's Will be done. The Lord
giveth and the Lord taketh away. Blessed be His Holy Name for ever
and ever, Amen. Burton with his usual affectionate consideration for us
sent his carriage for us and came himself and would not quit till he took
us both away to Persse Lodge, where your mother still remains and to
whence I shall return tomorrow.[67]

Poor fellow, his mild and very unoffensive manners caused him to
have many friends and the general regret for his death is very great.
Burton feels it very much and says that during the five years he was at
Newcastle he never had cause to find fault with him. Such is the uncer-
tainty of this life that we can reckon upon < . . . >. If he had lived he
would have < . . . > the full possessor of the Ho< . . . > where you
my Child were < . . . > my name it would be a bit < . . . > to see him
at the head < . . . > of the establishment. Whi< . . . >. What is to be
done < . . . > but I would suppose < . . . > to quit the Post Office and
his other pursuits and take charge of Newcastle. His illness was short.
He complained in the morning but thought it was an illness in his head
to which he was subject. He sent for leeches and took castor oil and
when the latter began to < . . . > as he thought but it was the < . . . >
cholera that he was seized with and therefore he would not let help
come to his aid 'till it was too late. I did not know till now that he had
the greatest dread of this disease, a presentiment that he would not
escape. As a small token of my affection and as tribute to his work I

purpose to put a small marble flag up in our pew and the wall of the
Church expressive of our regret and of his virtues.

I had a long letter from Mr. Morris from Lord Clanmorris, New
Brook. If Henry was his own child he could not < . . . > with more
regret < . . . > and if he were < . . . > he could not seek with < . . . >
kindness to soothe the affections < . . . > Mother and I are in < . . . >
was greatly shocked < . . . > moment he heard < . . . > post a letter
from < . . . > to invite to him to < . . . > some days with him.

There is a vacancy here in the general office of a Surveyor. It is £600
per year. Lord Clanmorris, Lord Howth and the Marquis Clanricarde
are using their interest in his favour.[68] Matty is pretty well considering
her situation and < . . . > they

[*part of the page is missing here, and the remainder of the letter is badly torn*]

does. She will be [confined?] < . . . > Sally too about the same < . . .
> I purpose to ask her < . . . > my house. I will take her and keep her
'till she is well.

I shall be most anxious <to?> hear from you all, so < . . . > my
children away from < . . . >. Cholera rages with a devastating < . . . >
makes me shudder at the < . . . > all I have now embarked < . . . >
States. May God bless you < . . . >Boy, and write to me frequently
< . . . > in the Divine Mercy to < . . . > you all, and with love to
< . . . > remain my Dearest Theophilus < . . . > loving and beloved
< . . . > ever affectionate < . . . >

H. S. Persse

No account has any of < . . . > the friends of the < . . . > and many
others < . . . >.

Letter 22

[*undated fragment, probably October 1832*]

each of the performers has two wands, with which the hoops are caught and kept in motion across the room, and a good performer will cast the small hoop through the large one while it is flying though the air. But the beauty of this game is the *attitudes*. Only think of a fine girl, her person beautifully attired, her hair in flowing ringlets and graceful curls, her right leg advanced from her body, her left fallen back, her person rather reclining somewhat backwards, her bosom projecting forward, a wand in each hand catching and throwing off in the graceful manner the hoops to her play fellow. In this position, with her arms unfolded, the blush of rosy health excited by exercise animating her countenance so as to make her appear as the emblem of happiness and beauty that I am sure if Mr. Edwards could see his Daughters thus engaged that he would burn the mill and roar out 'Free trade and the Graces for ever' and for the future take his fabrics and his fashions from Europe. Then the evenings could be spent with the Piano, and with Waltzing finish the night — when all might sing, that 'love was Liberty and Natural Law'. For what is Liberty if Free men are to be always at Work? Better leave this drudgery to the White Negroes in Europe and there keep your work shops and be [no] longer Slaves in reality, and only freemen in theory.

Stephen Creagh's Grandmother is dead. He expects £600 by her, but the Will is not open yet. He says if he gets that money and £800 settled by his Father that he and Sally would go to New York and give up the Post Office. I hope he may get relief, for he has been a great burthen upon your Mother and me.

I was at Persse Lodge for three weeks. I brought back two of Matty's little girls, dear little children, one 2 in November, the other 3 years old in November, Maria and Fanny. They are very fond of me. You never saw children so well brought up as all Matty's. She is as good a Mother and Wife as she was a Daughter or a Sister. I have now five servant maids in my house. What will your wife say to this! I sent for Kelly's people, told them what you said, and they are preparing a long letter to him.

At Glenascaul, a village near where Kelly lived, 16 persons died in one week. It is very bad here still. About 1000 took ill and 500 died. All those that are let out get new clothes. For sake of these, many take emetics, fain sickness and risk life for a nice suit of covering. But your newspapers know this for it is an astounding fact. I know of hundreds to commit crime to get to jail to be fed, but I never thought the[y] would face Cholera for clothing.

I expect either a [short?] terrier or a pup to go out by this conveyance. Heffernan proposes to work a year for you in lieu of his passage. I send you a package of newspapers.

The Cholera very bad today. Forty new [cases] last night at the moment we thought it was quitting us. It is a terrible scourge. God be praised I am blessed in not losing any of my family at home or abroad.

We just heard from Sally his Grandmother left Stephen but £350. He is quite disappointed. Fifteen persons already detected of drinking Tobacco juice boiled in milk to give them all the appearance of Cholera [*illegible*] that they might get into the Hospital to get food and clothing, as upon recovery the old clothing is burnt and new supplied.

[*The* Connacht Journal *for 31 October 1833 reports HSP's death as having taken place the previous day, though other reports suggest he may have died on 26 October.*]

Notes to Introduction

1   Cormac Ó Gráda 'Poverty, Population, and Agriculture, 1801–45' in W. E. Vaughan (ed.), *A New History of Ireland*, v *Ireland under the Union, I: 1801–70* (Oxford, 1989) pp. 108, 112.

2   Direct citations from HSP's letters are identified by the letter L followed by the number of the letter as given in the text. Unpublished correspondence cited here is in possession of Mary Louise Persse, Hamden, Connecticut, unless otherwise noted.

3   Lady Morgan, *The Wild Irish Girl* (London & New York, 1986 ed.), p. 8. Morgan's description of the prototypical 'Irish cabin' would become a stock feature in Anglo-Irish novels and Irish travel works through the mid-century and beyond. Hely Dutton's *Statistical and Agricultural Survey of the County of Galway* (Dublin, 1824) gives a similarly bleak portrait of life in the region dating to precisely the period of HSP's letters. For some account of possible reasons for the discrepancy between travellers' accounts of poverty and empirical evidence, noted by Cormac Ó Gráda among others, see Tim O'Neill, 'Minor Famines and Relief in Galway, 1815–1925' in Raymond Gillespie and Gerard Moran (eds), *Galway: History and Society* (forthcoming).

4   See J. G. Simms, 'Connacht in the Eighteenth Century', *Irish Historical Studies*, xi, (1958–59), pp. 116–33.

5   M. D. de Burgh Collins Persse, *De Burgh Fitzpatrick Persse (1840–1921) and his Family: An Essay in Anglo-Irish and Australian History, Part 1* (privately printed, 1971), p. 8.

6   James Hardiman, *The History of the Town and County of the Town of Galway, from the Earliest Period to the Present Time, 1820* (Galway, 1958 ed.), pp. 199–201.

7   Quoted in David Beers Quin, *The Elizabethans and the Irish* (Ithaca, 1966), p. 133.

8   Depositions of Rev. Edward Persse (9 Feb. 1641) and his servant Shane Bane (10 Feb. 1643), reproduced in *The Persse Story* (privately printed, New Haven, 1988) pp. 78–9.

9   Capoch, Downings and Clane, all in Co. Kildare.

10   Robert succeeded his father at Capoch, and became vicar at Straffan and Currach, also in Co. Kildare.

11   *The Persse Story*, pp. 78–9.

12   Ibid.

13   See J. P. Prendergast, *The Cromwellian Settlement of Ireland* (Dublin, 1922 ed.); J. G. Simms, *The Williamite Confiscation in Ireland, 1690–1703* (London, 1956).

14   Jerome Fahey, *The History and Antiquities of the Diocese of Kilmacduagh* (Dublin, 1893), p. 322.

15   Elizabeth Coxhead, *Lady Gregory: A Literary Portrait* (London, 1961), pp. 1–2.

As Coxhead observes, the dean was, at least as far as this legend went, 'a maligned man', since there were apparently 'other reasons for the plate's disappearance'.

16   Historical Manuscripts Commission, *Calendar of the Manuscripts of the Marquess of Ormonde, K.P., preserved at Kilkenny Castle*, new series, vi (London, 1911), p. 461.

17   Coxhead, *Lady Gregory*, p. 1.

18   The property is referred to as 'Rocksborough, otherwise Gregerosty' in a deed drawn up by William Persse and others in 1757 (reproduced in *The Persse Story*, p. 99); see also Coxhead, *Lady Gregory*, p. 1.

19   Lady Gregory, 'An Emigrant's Notebook' (unpublished memoir): Special Collections, Woodruff Library, Emory University.

20   U. H. Hussey de Burgh, *The Landowners of Ireland: An Alphabetical List of the Owners of Estates of 500 Acres or £500 Valuation and Upwards, in Ireland* (Dublin, 1878), pp. 365–6.

21   'Memoirs of the Hibernian Hero and Miss P —— m', *Town and Country Magazine*, v (1773), pp. 233–8.

22   W. B. Yeats, *Autobiographies* (Macmillan, 1955 ed.), p. 392.

23   Coxhead, *Lady Gregory*, pp. 10, 2.

24   Mary Lou Kohfeldt, *Lady Gregory: The Woman Behind the Irish Renaissance* (New York, 1985), p. 35.

25   Richard Lewis, *The Dublin Guide* (Dublin 1787), p. 59, quoted in James Mitchell, 'Colonel William Persse', *Journal of the Galway Archaeological and Historical Society*, xxx (1963), p. 79.

26   R. F. Foster, *Modern Ireland, 1600–1972* (London, 1988), p. 246.

27   Address reported in *Dublin Evening Post*, 13 Sept. 1781, quoted in Mitchell, 'Colonel William Persse', p. 53.

28   C. H. Wilson, *A Compleat Collection of the Resolutions of the Volunteers* (Dublin, 1782), i, 1–4, quoted in Mitchell, 'Colonel William Persse', p. 56.

29   Mitchell, 'Colonel William Persse', pp. 79–80.

30   ibid., p. 89.

31   George Washington Papers, ccxli: Library of Congress, Washington, D.C.; first published in Mitchell, 'Colonel William Persse', p. 87.

32   Mitchell, 'Colonel William Persse', p. 85.

33   Quoted ibid., p. 87.

34   Henry Stratford Persse leased an existing flour mill, also located on Nuns' Island, in 1811, but by then had already built a 'New Flour Mill' on adjoining property. See Marguerite Hayes-McCoy, 'The Eyre Documents in University College Galway', *Journal of the Galway Archaeological and Historical Society*, xxiii (1949), pp. 148–9. Persse's distillery operated until 1914, latterly selling its products under a trademark which included 1815 as the date of its founding.

35 'Galway Postal History', *Journal of the Galway Archaeological and Historical Society*, xlvii (1995), p. 221.

36 Hardiman, *Galway*, p. 327. Like the Nuns' Island distillery, Newcastle House was eventually acquired by University College, Galway, and was demolished during a recent expansion of the campus. The property was owned by HSP's brother Robert.

37 Kerby Miller, *Emigrants and Exiles: Ireland and the Irish Exodus to North America* (Oxford, 1985), p. 103. More recently, however, David Fitzpatrick has argued that emigration in the early nineteenth century involved a broader range in social, regional and religious terms than has previously been thought, and that Catholics may have dominated by the 1820s and 1830s. See David Fitzpatrick, 'Emigration, 1801–70' in *New History of Ireland*, v, 562–622.

38 The severity of the impact of the Union with Great Britain and of post-Waterloo taxation on the Irish economy is much debated. Nationalist writers such as George O'Brien, whose trilogy of commercial histories written between 1919 and 1921 were enormously influential during the early years of Irish independence, described the early decades of the nineteenth century in almost apocalyptic terms, reserving special scorn for imperialist policy-makers in London. These views have been repeatedly dismissed as counterfactual by empirical historians, whose figures on pork exports, rent rolls, butter production and so on present a much brighter portrait of Irish life than that of contemporary observers such as HSP. As Cormac Ó Gráda has observed, it is always dangerous to attend too closely to the complaints of Irish farmers or landlords, 'then as now effective propagandists'. The available statistics can, of course, be used to buttress radically differing theories. Ó Gráda, for instance, suggests that the closure of Ireland's parliament and the transfer of its various dependencies to London may have been more than compensated for in economic terms by fresh inloads of free-spending troopers sent over to Ireland for the maintenance of order. This analysis, however, disregards the psychological impact of the closure on the country, as evinced by the depression felt by men such as HSP's father, William Persse. The Act of Union neither destroyed the Irish economy nor reduced cottiers to an unprecedented new degree of serfdom, as hard line nationalists like O'Brien have argued. However, Irish debt did soar, its economy slowed, taxation rose (though even after the amalgamation of the exchequers in 1817 Irish taxes remained *lower* than those in Britain), and Dublin began its decline to the status of a provincial city. See Cormac Ó Gráda, *Ireland: A New Economic History* (Oxford, 1994), pp. 44–6, 74, 158–62; Foster, *Modern Ireland*, pp. 320–25; David S. Johnson and Liam Kennedy, 'National Historiography and the Decline of the Irish Economy' in Seán Hutton and Paul Stewart (eds), *Ireland's Histories: Aspects of State, Society and Ideology* (London, 1991), pp. 11–35.

39   This mix of 'rich and poor', landlords and 'working people' observed by HSP
      adds support to David Fitzpatrick's argument regarding the demographics of emi-
      gration in the early nineteenth century (see note 37 above). H. D. Inglis, writing
      of a shipload of seventy bound for America from Galway in 1834, noted that they
      'were mostly agricultural labourers, possessed of very little beyond their passage
      money . . . I found no Protestant amongst those with whom I conversed.' H. D.
      Inglis, *Ireland in 1834* (2 vols, London, 1834), ii, 137.

40   Miller, *Emigrants and Exiles*, p. 201.

41   Symptomatically, HSP seems not to have been a Freemason, unlike many other
      members of his family. His second son, Henry Sadleir Persse, was a founding
      member of Lodge 9 in Galway in 1825, as was Henry's 'lick plate' brother Robert
      Dudley from 1836. HSP's brother Robert was a member of Lodge 14 in Galway
      from 1814.

42   Agrarian violence had been a constant in Irish life, dating back to the clan dis-
      putes and warfare of the 'heroic' period. Cattle-raids, nocturnal theft, and the use
      of threats, boasts and disguise are all familiar themes in Irish literature and tradi-
      tion, from the *Táin Bó Cuailgne* to Pastorini's *General History of the Christian Church*,
      a 'millenarian' concoction published in 1771 (with which HSP was probably
      familiar) that predicted the bloody demise of Protestantism quite precisely to the
      year 1825. The character of rural violence to which HSP refers here and in other
      letters dates from the mid–1700s, when impoverished peasants began to organ-
      ise loosely in Munster in order to protest and resist tithes, evictions and low
      wages. This agitation contributed to the rebellion of 1798, and was ruthlessly
      repressed, only to reappear sporadically after the Union, again predominantly in
      the south and south-west regions of the country. These secret societies — known
      as Whiteboys, Ribbonmen, Carders, Caravats and Rockites — varied in menace
      and purpose, but were by and large anti-Protestant, anti-landlord and anti-British.
      During the first quarter of the nineteenth century there were only brief periods
      when their activities were dormant, and events such as those HSP refers to were
      more often in the order of pitched battles than isolated instances of thuggery. In
      February 1822 three hundred 'Whiteboys' awaited trial, mostly in Munster.
      British authorities, in little doubt as to their probable conviction, anticipated sen-
      tencing by building gibbets and arranging for transportations. One prisoner in
      ten was sentenced to death. Daniel O'Connell, though he defended many indi-
      viduals involved in such crimes, saw little political benefit in their activities. Some
      historians now feel his drive for Catholic Emancipation turned many small farm-
      ers and peasants away from the course of violent confrontation. See S. J. Con-
      nolly, 'Mass Politics and Sectarian Conflict, 1823–30' in *New History of Ireland*, v,
      pp. 80–84; James S. Donnelly, Jr, 'Pastorini and Captain Rock: Millenarianism
      and Sectarianism in the Rockite Movement of 1821–24' in Samuel Clark and J. S.

Donnelly, Jr (eds) *Irish Peasants: Violence and Political Unrest, 1780–1914* (Madison & Manchester, 1983); Galen Broeker, *Rural Disorder and Police Reform in Ireland, 1823–36* (London, 1970).

43　One exception is the series of reports filed by Henry Brearly from Galway from late May 1822 on behalf on the London Tavern Relief Committee. These attest clearly to the fact that fever and extreme hardship were widespread, and noted that 'many' people had 'perished through hunger in Connemara', but they give little detail of mortality rates in Galway city, although they do confirm that large numbers had flocked there from outlying regions in search of relief. The reports were sufficiently grave for the British parliament to organise relief in response. See O'Neill, 'Minor Famines and Relief in Galway'.

44　As noted in the text accompanying his letter of September 1832, HSP's totals for death and sickness square closely with those available from the Board of Health tallies during the period. However, this may simply evidence his reading of these tallies rather than confirm his accuracy as an independent observer.

45　HSP's personal involvement with the relief operations lends significant support to his claims about the extent of the famine, but at the same time his evident shock at the sight of people dying like 'rotten sheep' in the streets and his disgust at both Ascendancy complacency and British *laissez-faire* politics underscore the extent to which his accounts are not impartial or simply forensic.

46　See *A Catalogue of Printed Books formerly in the Library at Coole* (Sotheby & Co., London), 20–21 Mar. 1972), esp. items 92, 103, 104, 112, 182, 220, 228, 284, 290, 299, 382, 424.

47　David Fitzpatrick, *Oceans of Consolation: Personal Accounts of Irish Migration to Australia* (Ithaca, 1994), p. 503. This work gives extensive consideration (see esp. pp. 467–534) to the conventions of letter exchange — from the ceremonies of communication, to the influence of obligation in kinship networks, to the impact of the inevitable delay between composition, receipt and (uncertain) reply in letter-writing — all of which factors leave their mark on HSP's correspondence.

48　The *New York Herald* was a weekly digest first published by Michael Burnham around 1804 in conjunction with the considerably larger daily, the *Evening Post*, founded in 1801 and largely written by its eventual editor William Coleman. These papers were initially financed by, and espoused the Federalist viewpoints of, Alexander Hamilton and John Jay, and warmly supported DeWitt Clinton during his presidential campaign of 1812 and his governorship of New York. Coleman's *Herald* should not be confused with the *New York Herald* of 1835, founded by Scotsman James Gordon Bennett, one of nineteenth-century America's most successful (and wealthy) journalists. See W. L. Stone, 'Newspapers and Magazines' in James Grant (ed.), *The Memorial History of the City of New York* (New York, 1893), pp. 145–50; Allan Nevins, *The Evening Post: A Century of Journalism* (New York, 1922), p. 20.

49   Howard Robinson, *The British Post Office* (Princeton, 1948), p. 178. See also pp.179–80 for commentary on the widespread abuse of franking privileges by Irish Post Office officials during the period. With overseas letters, senders typically had to pay part of the cost, meeting the charges for reaching the point of sailing in the case of mail sent by packet, and in the case of the cheaper 'ship letters' having to meet the full cost of postage in advance.

50   According to Máiréad Reynolds, *A History of the Irish Post Office* (Dublin, 1983), p. 40, abuse of the franking system by Post Office officials was rife until 1821, when 'stringent regulations to stop the abuse' were enacted, although HSP evidently managed to evade these new regulations for at least some time. The sending of private ship letters not through the Post Office was at this point deemed to be illegal contraband, but was not effectively prevented until 1837.

51   *Connacht Journal*, 4 Oct. 1832.

52   'Atticus' [pseudonym of DeWitt Clinton], *Remarks on the Proposed Canal from Lake Erie to the Hudson River* (New York, 1816), p. 884.

53   Ibid., p. 877.

54   David Maldwyn Ellis, *Landlords and Farmers in the Hudson–Mohawk Region, 1790–1850* (Ithaca, 1946), p. 134, quoted in Ronald E. Shaw, *Erie Water West: A History of the Erie Canal, 1792–1854* (Lexington, 1966), p. 7.

55   David Hosack, *Memoir of DeWitt Clinton: with an Appendix containing Numerous Documents illustrative of the Principal Events of his Life* (New York, 1829), p. 257.

56   Shaw, *Erie Water West*, p. 274.

57   William Otis Hotchkiss, *Early Days of the Erie Canal — Adventures in Statesmanship and Canal Transport* (Princeton, 1940), p. 10.

58   'Peter Ploughshare', *Considerations against continuing the Great Canal West of the Seneca; Addressed to the Members-Elect of the Legislature of New York* (Utica, 1819) pp. 3–4.

59   'Atticus', *Remarks on the Proposed Canal*, p. 881.

60   The late nineteenth-century historian Henry Adams, whose family were long-standing detractors of Clinton, heaped scorn on what he considered to have been a hypocritical and egocentric election campaign against Madison: 'No canvass for the Presidency was ever less creditable than that of DeWitt Clinton in 1812. Seeking war votes for the reason that he favored more vigorous prosecution of the war; asking support from peace Republicans because Madison had plunged the country into war without preparation; bargaining for Federalist votes as the price of bringing about peace; or coquetting with all parties in the atmosphere of bribery in bank charters — Clinton strove to make up a majority which had no element of union but himself and money.' See Henry Adams, 'The First Administration of James Madison, 1809–1813' in *The History of the United States*, ii (New York, 1890), p. 410.

61 Nathan Miller, *The Enterprise of a Free People: Aspects of Economic Development in New York during the Canal Period, 1792–1838* (Ithaca, 1962), p. 85.

62 Herman Melville, *Moby Dick, or The Whale*, (2 vols, London, 1922 ed.), i, 315 (Chapter 54: 'The Town-Ho's Story').

63 Philip Freneau (1752–1832) in New Brunswick *Fredonian*, 8 Aug. 1822, cited in Lionel D. Wyld, *Low Bridge! Folklore and the Erie Canal* (Syracuse, 1962), pp. 2, 119.

64 Francis P. Kimball, *New York — The Canal State* (Albany, 1937), p. xiii, quoted in Wyld, *Low Bridge!*, p. 9.

65 A. Levasseur, *Lafayette in America in 1824 and 1825*, trans. John D. Godman (Philadelphia, 1829), p. 7, cited in Wyld, *Low Bridge!*, p. 39.

66 Shaw, *Erie Water West*, p. 261.

67 'Atticus', *Remarks on the Proposed Canal*, p. 875.

68 Nathaniel Hawthorne, 'Sketches from Memory' in *Mosses from an Old Manse*, (*Works*, ii (Boston, 1882)), as quoted in Wyld, *Low Bridge!*, p. 128.

69 William Dean Howells, *Their Wedding Journey* (Boston, 1872), p. 85, as quoted in Wyld, *Low Bridge!*, p. 128.

70 Washington to Governor George Clinton, 25 Nov. 1784, in *The Writings of George Washington from the Original Manuscript Sources, 1745–1799*, ed. John C. Fitzpatrick, xxvii (Washington, 1938), p. 501.

71 'Atticus', *Remarks on the Proposed Canal*, p. 877.

72 See Julian Gwyn, *The Enterprising Admiral: The Personal Fortune of Admiral Sir Peter Warren* (Montreal, 1974); also *The Royal Navy and North America: The Warren Papers, 1736–1752* (London, 1973).

73 Charles Johnstone, *Chrysal, or The Adventures of a Guinea* (London, 1767), iii, 135–66.

74 For Johnson see Arthur Pound, *Johnson of the Mohawks* (New York, 1930); James Thomas Flexner, *Mohawk Baronet: Sir William Johnson* (New York, 1959); Francis Taormina, *William Johnson* (Schenectady, 1993); also *Papers of Sir William Johnson*, ed. Alexander C. Flick (Albany, 1925), iii, 139–55, 163; iv, 151. See also Alan Taylor, *William Cooper's Town: Power and Persuasion on the Frontier of the Early American Republic* (New York, 1995).

75 Miller, *Enterprise of a Free People*, pp. 99–111.

76 Philip Hone, merchant, to DeWitt Clinton, 9 Oct. 1826, quoted ibid., p. 91.

77 When I landed in sweet Philadelphia,
 The weather was pleasant and clear,
 I did not stay long in the city,
 So quickly I shall let you hear,
 I did not stay long in the city,
 For it happened to be in the fall,

I never reefed a sail in my rigging,
'Till I anchored out on the canal.

When I came to this wonderful empire,
It filled me with the greatest surprise,
To see such a great undertaking,
On the like I never opened my eyes,
To see full a thousand brave fellows,
At work amongst mountains so tall,
To dig through the vallies so level,
Through rocks for to cut a canal.

I entered with them for a season,
My monthly pay for to draw,
And being in very good humor,
I often sang Erin go Bragh,
Our provision it was very plenty,
To complain we'd no reason at all.,
I had money in every pocket,
While working on the canal.

For complete lyrics see *The American Vocalist* (New York, 1853), pp. 137–38, quoted in Wyld, *Low Bridge!*, pp. 80–81.

78   DeWitt Clinton Papers, Columbia University.

79   Samuel Eliot Morrison and Henry Steele Commager, *The Growth of the American Republic* (New York, 1950), p. 426.

80   Percy Ashley, *Modern Tariff History* (New York, 1970) pp. 133–50; see also Dall W. Forsyth, *Taxation and Political Change in the Young Nation, 1781–1833* (New York, 1977), pp. 62–106; George R. Taylor (ed.), *The Great Tariff Debate* (Boston, 1953); Jonathan J. Pincus, *Pressure Groups and Politics in Antebellum Tariffs* (New York, 1977); Charles W. Wiltse, *The New Nation, 1800–1845* (New York, 1961), pp. 72–5.

81   *The Message of the Governor to the Legislature of the State of New York on the Opening of the Session, 4 January 1825* (Albany, 1825), pp. 17–18.

82   Hosack, *Memoir of DeWitt Clinton*, p. 875.

83   George Dangerfield, *The Awakening of American Nationalism, 1815–1828* (New York, 1965), p. 119; *The Papers of John C. Calhoun*, ix: *1824–1825*, ed. W. Edwin Hemphill (Columbia, 1976), p. 396. See also Robert V. Remini, *Martin Van Buren and the Making of the Democratic Party* (New York, 1970), pp. 6–7; Steven Siry, 'DeWitt Clinton and the American Political Economy: Sectionalism, Politics and

Republican Ideology, 1787–1828' (Ph.D. thesis, University of Cincinnati, 1977).

84 Deed, 5 Apr. 1831: Registry of Deeds, Montgomery County, New York.

85 'Atticus', *Remarks on the Proposed Canal*, p. 875. See also Daniel M. Friedenberg, *Life, Liberty and the Pursuit of Land: The Plunder of Early America* (Amherst, 1992); W. B. Rothenberg, *From Market-Places to a Market Economy: The Transformation of Rural Massachusetts, 1750–1850* (Chicago, 1992).

86 See Washington Frothingham, *History of Montgomery County* (Syracuse, 1892); also F. W. Beers & Co., *History of Montgomery and Fulton Counties, New York, with Illustrations Descriptive of Scenery, Private Residences, Public Buildings, Fine Blocks, and Important Manufactories* (New York, 1878).

87 Dudley Persse to Theophilus Persse, 5 Apr. 1826: in possession of Thomas Persse, Fonda, New York.

88 Tom Persse to Theophilus Persse, 4 Dec. 1841: ibid.

89 'I remember but seeing one before,' Jabez H. Hayden observed, referring to Irish labourers, in *Historical Sketches* (Windsor Locks, 1900), pp. 33–4.

90 Charles Dickens, *American Notes* (New York, 1985), pp. 33–4.

91 Edward E. Lanati, *A Brief Account of the Windsor Locks Canal* (Windsor Locks, 1976); see also *The Story of Windsor Locks, 1663–1976* (Windsor Locks, n.d.).

92 John Doggett, Jr, *Doggett's New York City Directory for 1850–1851* (New York, 1850), p. 396.

93 Harriet Amelia Lambert to Mary Anne (Mrs. Theophilus) Persse, 6 Sept. 1849.

94 Inventory, 1854: Probate Records, State Library, Hartford, Connecticut.

95 See J. Hammond Trumbull (ed.), *The Memorial History of Hartford County, Connecticut, 1633–1884* (Boston, 1886), p. 570; Davis Rich Dewey, *Financial History of the United States* (London, 1903), pp. 263–5; George W. Van Vleck, *The Panic of 1857: An Analytical Study* (New York, 1943).

96 Insolvency declaration, 24 Dec. 1857: Probate Records, State Library, Hartford, Connecticut.

97 *Hartford Courant*, 1 Apr. 1861.

98 Hartford *Daily Times*, 2, 4 Apr. 1861.

99 J.H. Beers & Co., *Commemorative Biographical Record of Hartford County, Connecticut, containing Biographical Sketches of Prominent and Representative Citizens, and Many of the Early Settler Families* (Chicago, 1901), p. 208.

100 *Denver Daily News*, 30 Jan. 1911.

101 E. B. McGuire, *Irish Whiskey* (Dublin, 1973), p. 360. An undated letter from Anne Persse, HSP's widow, written *circa* 1852, alludes briefly to Thomas's later career and family strains relating to HSP's old businesses: 'You will of course hear from Dudley that Tom is now out of the distillery. I do not know all the particulars but I know enough to make me sad and to make me know that Tom has been most ungrateful to his sister [Mattie] and her husband [Burton Persse].'

102 Thomas Moore Persse to Theophilus Persse, 4 Dec. 1841.

103 An undated letter from Anne Persse (*circa* 1852) shows that they remained in Galway, and that Sally Persse Creagh had by that date died, leaving eleven children with 'no property'.

104 Undated letter from Anne Persse (*circa* 1852).

Notes to Narrative

1   HSP's eldest brother, Robert Persse (d. 1850), master of Roxborough, the main Persse estate.

2   The island of Hispaniola (now the Dominican Republic and Haiti) and especially the port of Santo Domingo had become bywords for the atrocities committed by Spanish slave traders in recent decades. British diplomatic pressure had led in 1820 to a Spanish agreement to terminate slave-trading.

3   HSP's inquisitiveness about conditions in America is evident in this letter in his renewed requests for information, and his obviously energetic acquisition of newspapers, maps and other published materials. William Darby's *Tour from the City of New York to Detroit* (New York, 1819) covered the region his emigrant sons had traversed. Darby had earlier published other American regional guide-books partly intended, as was this one, for new immigrants.

4   'Wirra Sthru!' is a phonetic English rendering of a Gaelic exclamation meaning 'O Mary, it is a pity!'

5   John Lambert (b. *c.* 1800), the second son of HSP's 'Aunt Betty' Lambert (see headnote to Letter 2).

6   Richard St George (1765–1851), 2nd Bart, was William's cousin through the marriage of HSP's sister Sarah to Sir Richard St George, 1st Bart, of Woodsgift (d. 1789).

7   Merlin Park, three miles east of Galway city, an estate then owned by Charles Blake, became later in the century the home of Lady Gregory's sister, Arabella Persse, following her marriage to William Waithman. It was bought by the Irish government in the 1940s under a compulsory purchase order and demolished to provide a site for a new Galway hospital.

8   John Blakeney (d. 1858), a cousin of HSP.

9   Judge Moore was the father-in-law of HSP's cousin William Persse (1788–1849).

10 Robert Parsons Persse (d. 1829) was also HSP's cousin, being the eldest son of William Persse's younger brother Parsons, and master of the Castleboy estate. For the complex circumstances surrounding the eventual succession of his estate — involving lunacy proceedings, the claims of an illegitimate son, and charges of suppression of documents — see Letter 15.

11   Laurence Parsons (1758–1841), 2nd Earl of Rosse, was a Persse family conection
      via the marriage of HSP's grandfather, Robert Persse, to Elizabeth Parsons, sister
      of the 1st Lord Rosse, in 1727, a connection sufficiently valuable for the Persses
      to have used Parsons repeatedly as a given name in subsequent generations. See
      also Introduction for Rosse's role in the Irish mail service.

12   Power le Poer Trench (1770–1839), Archbishop of Tuam 1819–39.

13   Richard Shannon's *Practical Treatise on Brewing, Distilling and Rectification* was pub-
      lished in 1805. HSP's 'volume' on brewing was presumably a private manual
      compiled for use in his own brewery and distillery, and was not published.

14   The 'disturbances' in England HSP refers to included riots by agricultural labour-
      ers in Norfolk in early March 1822, while riots had also taken place in Paris, first
      in protest at the preaching of visiting missionaries, and then against coercive
      police measures against the protestors. HSP was at this point evidently willing to
      see such widespread troubles as evidence of the breakdown of Western Europe
      following the failed military and political climaxes of the previous decade.

15   Lady Morgan (1776?–1859), born Sydney Owenson, was, with Maria Edge-
      worth, one of the most popular Irish novelists of the period. Her treatment of
      Irish nationality and culture in novels such as *The Wild Irish Girl* (1806) and *O'Don-
      nel* (1814) would have appealed to HSP in inviting a more informed and sympa-
      thetic view of Irish affairs by English audiences. Frances Wright's *Views of Society
      and Manners in America,* a series of letters she had written home over 1818–20,
      was published in 1821. Her liberal views, influenced by Tom Paine and Robert
      Owen, and her anti-slavery stance would have particularly appealed to HSP.

16   HSP probably alludes to Swift's poem 'The Lady's Dressing Room', an inventory
      of bedroom disarray and sordidness which belies its mistress's carefully made-up
      public face.

17   Thomas Taylor of Castle Taylor, County Galway, who had married HSP's mater-
      nal aunt, Mary Blakeney, in 1759.

18   John Melish (1771–1822) published numerous volumes of maps and topograph-
      ical description of the U.S.A., including *The Traveller's Directory* (1815).

19   Frank and Burton ('Burty') Persse were HSP's two youngest sons.

20   Thomas Erskine (1750–1823), youngest son of the 10th Earl of Buchan, served
      in the navy as a midshipman until he was eighteen, and then in the army until he
      was twenty-four. After switching to the law, he was called to the bar in 1778 and
      became Lord Chancellor in 1806.

21   The recently crowned George IV (d. 1830) had visited Ireland for three weeks
      from mid-August 1821. The 'welcome buttons' were sovereigns specially minted
      for the occasion. HSP mentions in Letter 3 that he has enclosed nine sovereigns
      in that mailing.

22   The voyages of explorer James Cook (1728–79) first introduced Westerners to

the indigenous cultures of Australia, Hawaii and the Pacific Islands.

23   Richard Sadleir (1785–1845), Clement Sadleir's son.

24   William Worth Newenham, who married HSP's sister Elizabeth (see Introduction). Their son Robert Newenham is mentioned in subsequent letters.

25   The tax exiles HSP lists here were among the major Galway landlords of the time. Richard Gregory of Coole (d. 1839) was grand-uncle of Sir William Gregory (1816–92), later husband of Augusta Persse (Lady Gregory). Robert O'Hara of Raheen was connected to the Gregorys through the marriage of his daughter to Richard Gregory's nephew. 'Mr. French [*sic*] of Monivea' was also a distant family connection, through the marriage of one of Dean Dudley Persse's grandsons into the Ffrench family. Frederic Trench (1755–1840) was created Lord Ashtown in 1800 in return for voting in favour of Union, his 'venality', in Jonah Barrington's summary, being extreme even in that season of conspicuous vote-selling. He was related to the Persses through his mother, born Mary Sadleir. Charles Bingham (1796–1829), 2nd Baron Clanmorris, was likewise a family connection, having married Sarah Lambert, daughter of HSP's 'Aunt Betty' (see Letter 2) in 1816.

26   British Passenger Acts, particularly from 1803 on, though ostensibly enacted to improve conditions on crowded emigrant ships, in fact served to discriminate against American shipping interests and to prevent the loss of trained artisans to a rival economy. Forced to carry fewer passengers per ship, American carriers raised the price of trans-Atlantic tickets. Most Irish emigrants in this period consequently travelled to North America on Canadian timber vessels at half the cost. In 1822, for instance, 8,000 immigrants landed in Quebec, as opposed to only 2,000 in the United States. Most of these arrivals, however, subsequently made their way south to the American republic.

27   The Lombard Barracks were situated on Lombard and Bridge Street, Galway, just across the river from HSP's businesses on Nuns' Island.

28   Finvarra, king of the *sídhe*, reputedly lived on Cruachmaa, or Knockma, a hill near Tuam, County Galway.

29   HSP's remarks both in this and later letters about contraction in the money supply pick up on the widespread contemporary anxiety about deflation. The *Annual Register* had reported in June 1822 that the price of gold had fallen to below the cost of the mint price, 'a circumstance which has not taken place since the year 1797'.

30   HSP here refers to a widely publicised scandal which had just occurred in which the Hon. Percy Jocelyn, Bishop of Clogher, was caught *in flagrante delicto* with a private of the foot guards in a back room of a London public house.

31   Theophilus's 'Fonda' was a village situated on the north bank of the Mohawk River. Four miles away, and 400 feet higher in elevation, lay Johnstown. Fonda

had long been settled, first by Indians, then by Dutch, and later German, farmers. The French missionary Jogues was tortured and martyred here in 1646, an event described in the *Jesuit Relations* and by Francis Parkman in his monumental *France and England in North America*. 'Langsine', presumably, is another geographic location and not a person.

32 HSP's contemptuous mention of 'Peelers' refers to the permanent constabulary established by Sir Robert Peel when Chief Secretary for Ireland 1812–18. Nominally organised for the preservation of order and property, the constabulary was largely employed at the outset in suppressing Catholic agitations. While HSP was no admirer of Daniel O'Connell, he may well have agreed with the latter's remark that 'Peel's smile was like a silver plate on a coffin.'

33 For William Persse's two surviving letters to George Washington see James Mitchell, 'Colonel William Persse', *Journal of the Galway Archaeological and Historical Society*, xxx (1963), pp. 80–84. Evidence survives to confirm that HSP's sons did publish the letter to his father he mentions here in the New York press, but not when or where. Washington's death in 1799 had unleashed a torrent of biographical works and pamphlets, introducing many of the fictions (such as the cherry tree incident) subsequently so familiar to schoolchildren in the United States. HSP most likely refers here to the collected works of Mason Locke Weems, whose *Life of George Washington, with Curious Anecdotes Equally Honorable to Himself and Exemplary to His Young Countrymen* (printed in numerous editions) was a compendium of absurd biographical musings. John Marshall's *Life of George Washington* (1804), 'a great, heavy book', was also widely read, though one British critic complained that 'one gets sick and tired of the very name of Washington before he gets half through these . . . prodigious . . . octavos'.

34 A statutory commission began inquiring into the workings of the Irish revenue service in 1821 and resulted in the fusing of the Irish department with and under the control of its British counterpart in 1823. The notorious window tax, first introduced in 1695, had by 1798 been reduced to cover only houses with six or more windows. In 1823 this was further reduced to five windows, with the tax finally being repealed in favour of a house tax in 1851.

35 A new Constabulary Bill introduced early in 1822 had provided for the organisation of a permanent police force in Ireland, with barony constables to be appointed by magistrates of the county they were to serve in.

36 Samuel Wade of Carrowmore was the father-in-law of HSP's brother Robert Parsons Persse, master of Roxborough.

37 'Your Uncle Burton' was in fact HSP's uncle, Burton Persse (1746–1831), known as 'The Irish Meynell' in acknowledgement of his status as the premier huntsman of Ireland. His famous hounds subsequently established the nucleus of the celebrated Galway Blazers, formally organised in 1839.

38   The books HSP promises to send include *The American Gardener* by William Cob-
      bett (1763–1835), first published in England in 1821, and *The New Horse-Hoing
      Husbandry; or, An Essay on the Principles of Tillage and Vegetation* by Jethro Tull
      (1674–1741), published in numerous editions since 1741, most recently in 1822
      with an introduction by Cobbett. Cobbett, now best known for his *Rural Rides*,
      was a liberal thinker, much influenced by Thomas Paine, who had spent several
      years in the USA, writing extensively on American democracy. HSP was clearly
      an enthusiast of Cobbett's proto-socialist philosophy. His exasperated remarks on
      the nature of the money supply and taxation in this letter almost certainly draw
      on Cobbett's essays *Paper Against Gold* of 1815–17, which stressed that poverty
      would inevitably increase under the existing system of taxation and paper cur-
      rency.

39   Warden Ffrench, a Catholic friend of HSP (see Letter 3), served as the principal
      benfactor of the Presentation Convent when it first opened in 1815 to serve the
      needs of 'poor, unprotected females'. The needlework produced there by some
      350 apprentice sewers was well regarded throughout Connacht.

40   HSP's wife's family, the Sadleirs, came from County Cork.

41   HSP's concern to arrange free delivery of his sons' letters via the Earl of Rosse
      reflects the considerable expense of mail delivery at this period. See Introduc-
      tion, p. 36–7.

42   'Prime Ministers cut[ting] their throats' alludes to the suicide of Lord
      Castlereagh, who killed himself with a penknife on 12 August 1822. Though For-
      eign Secretary rather than Prime Minister, he was widely regarded as being for
      all practical purposes the leader of Lord Liverpool's government. For the scandal
      of the bishop and the soldier see note 30.

43   Dudley Persse (1802–78) was HSP's nephew, being the eldest son of Robert
      Persse of Roxborough (which he would also inherit) and subsequently father of
      Lady Gregory.

44   Madame de Stael (1766–1817) was the most popular French novelist of the
      period.

45   I.e. on foot.

46   Joseph C. Yates, an Associate Justice on the New York Supreme Court, won a
      virtually uncontested election for Governor in 1822, at a period when DeWitt
      Clinton's popularity had ebbed precipitously over political matters unrelated to
      the Erie Canal. Yates, in his turn, displeased the electorate, and Clinton subse-
      quently regained office for a third term beginning in 1825.

47   During the so-called 'bottle riot' of 14 December 1822 the Lord Lieutenant of
      Ireland, Marquis Wellesley (1760–1842), had a bottle and other projectiles
      thrown at him during a performance at the Theatre Royal in Dublin by Orange-
      men enraged by his support for the cause of Catholic Emancipation. The incident

further inflamed already severe religious tensions. HSP's liberality and distrust of partisan loyalties of any stripe is obvious in his comments here.

48   Dudley had left Johnstown to apprentice himself to a merchant, possibly in Pattersonville, New York (HSP gives 'Paterston'), some twenty miles from Johnstown. HSP wonders hypothetically here how much Dudley might be able to save towards a business of his own between the ages of eighteen and twenty-one, but Dudley was probably already at least nineteen by this time.

49   Senator Daniel Webster had also made rhetorical reference to the *canaille* and serfs of Europe in his arguments *against* the tariff of 1824, suggesting that if such workers could produce iron at wages of seven cents a day, it was so much the better, and that American workers were better employed in other businesses: 'If we had an ignorant, idle, starving population, we might set up for the iron makers against the world.'

50   HSP's 'Holy Compact' refers to the Holy Alliance, proposed by Tsar Alexander I in 1815, whereby the monarchs of Russia, Austria and Prussia agreed to resolve international disputes by the light of 'Christian Charity' and 'the Word of the Most High'. Most contemporaries regarded the agreement as meaningless, with Castlereagh dismissing it as 'nonsense'. In HSP's usage, typical of many liberal thinkers of the time, the Holy Alliance stood for the *ancien régime*, superstitious religiosity and suppression of the individual. The Hartford Convention, an assembly of New England Federalists who opposed the war with Great Britain on moral and economic grounds, met in Connecticut's capitol on 14 December 1815, in largely secret session, causing great concern to President Madison. Though fuelled by cries of 'no impressment' and 'free trade on the open seas' — issues dear to the New England maritime states — the war was highly unpopular in the north-east The Convention was conceived to originate secession from a Union now run, participants considered, by a cabal of Virginia farmers and western frontiersmen who had never seen the Atlantic and knew nothing of commerce. To the relief of Madison, the Convention produced nothing after a month but a ream of rhetoric and an aura of subversion and cowardice from within that Federalists could henceforth never shake, an aspersion HSP echoes here.

51   'Fir-built frigates, manned by a handful of bastards and outlaws', the jaundiced assessment of American naval craft by an English journalist during the war of 1812, was a phrase widely quoted on both sides of the Atlantic.

52   In his idealised portrait of manufacturer and agriculturalist standing 'side by side', HSP quotes directly from Thomas Jefferson, whose 'conversion' to this equality of status was more political than heartfelt. HSP's analysis of Ulster's manufacturing success in the linen and cotton industries also seems idealised. In 1825, just one year after this letter, final tariff restrictions protecting Irish interests were removed, with generally disastrous results. British producers, themselves in the

midst of a depression, flooded the Irish market with inexpensive textiles. Kerby Miller has estimated that in just thirteen years, production decreased by 85 per cent. In that same period a quarter of Belfast's cotton mills closed, and linen manufacturers survived only through technological innovations that impacted severely on the workforce, particularly in the remote valleys of Ulster.

53   The contracts of apprenticeship between Everett Yates and Theophilus and Richard ended acrimoniously. In a letter to Richard shipped along in her father's parcel Mattie Persse wrote that 'We were all gratified with the account . . . of the family you are to live with. In fact. I am most happy that you made the change. All I wonder at is that you could have remained with the Yates so long.'

54   Walter ('Watt') Lambert (1795–1867) had just succeeded his father, HSP's uncle. 'Lady C., Betsey and Anna Maria' were Watt's three elder sisters, 'Lady C.' being Sarah, who had married the 2nd Baron Clanmorris in 1816.

55   Shittim wood, from the acacia tree, was reputedly the material used to make the Ark of the Covenant.

56   This was Robert Henry Persse (1806–84), second son of HSP's eldest brother, Robert Persse of Roxborough. His mother, Maria Wade of Fairfield, had died in 1810. Henry in fact remained in Ireland, married in 1828 and had eight surviving children, and briefly inherited the Castleboy estate following his father's committal that year, only to lose it in an acrimonious lawsuit with his own brother (see Letter 15 and note 60 below).

57   Eliza Persse was the third daughter of HSP's brother Robert Persse of Roxborough. She married Thomas Warren White in February 1825.

58   William Blakeney Persse, HSP's elder brother.

59   Theophilus's sister Mattie married HSP's cousin Burton de Burgh Persse (d. 1859) of Moyode Castle in November 1825. At Moyode she became an active proselytiser of the tenantry, building a Protestant day school — called 'The Nest' — 'to undermine the faith of local children' (according to the local Catholic priest). Such proselytising efforts provoked a renaissance of sorts at the Dominican friary at nearby Esker, which energised its 'hedge school' to counter what the poet Raftery called 'the men of false Bibles'.

60   Robert Parsons Persse of Castleboy was declared a lunatic and committed in 1828 following proceedings instituted by Dudley Persse (HSP's nephew, later Lady Gregory's father) on behalf of his father, Robert Persse. A struggle for legal control of the estate ensued between Dudley Persse and his second cousin, Burton Persse of Moyode, and, in due course, other claimants, including an illegitimate son of Robert Parsons Persse named George. Court cases over the estate took place in 1828–29, 1830, 1835–36, 1840 (at which point it was heard before the House of Lords), 1852 and 1856, with Dudley Persse managing to retain control of most of the property. Acrimony over the proceedings continued for decades

in the family, with the final exchanges being initiated late in the century by Captain Robert Persse, eldest son of Dudley's brother Robert, who privately published in 1894 an account of the decades of proceedings, *Castleboy: A Deed of Settlement Suppressed in a Court of Justice*. This pamphlet charged Dudley Persse with gross conflict of interest in initiating the lunacy proceedings against Robert Parsons Persse, and with suppressing or destroying a deed of 1807 which negated the covenants on which he had based his claim to the estate. The hostility spawned by the trials (and, presumably, embarrassment over the lunacy proceedings) is symptomatically apparent in the exclusion of Robert Parsons Persse from genealogical tables compiled for *Burke's Irish Family Records* and other publications by subsequent generations of Persses.

61 Richard Anderson's father was Joseph Anderson (1757–1837), a Senator for Tennessee 1797–1815, and Comptroller of the US Treasury 1815–36.

62 Theophilus married Mary Anne Edwards on 10 February 1829.

63 Fonda was originally called by the Indians *Cahaniaga* ('Stone in the Water'), here spelled phonetically by HSP as *Canandaigua*.

64 The custom of indentured servants trading a certain length of employment for ship passage to the New World was fast disappearing as a regular practice by the time of this letter, though in earlier decades the traffic had been significant and, in the eighteenth century, at times little better than slavery.

65 Theophilus's first child, Anne, was born on 29 March 1830.

66 Mattie Persse had had two daughters, Sarah and Maria, and one son, Burton (b. 1828), since her marriage in 1825.

67 HSP's uncle, Burton Persse (1746–1831) of Moyode.

68 Thomas St Lawrence (1803–74), 3rd Earl of Howth, had married the youngest daughter of the 3rd Earl of Clanricarde in 1826.

Index